Books in the series "Crafting your career in academia":

- Writing effective promotion applications (August 2022)
- Publishing in academic journals (November 2022)
- Creating social media profiles (February 2023)
- Measuring and improving research impact (May 2023)
- Using the Publish or Perish software (August 2023)

# Creating social media profiles

## Crafting your career in academia

Anne-Wil Harzing

Edition: March 2023

ISBN 978-1-7396097-4-0 (paperback, black & white)

Published by Tarma Software Research Ltd, UK

| | |
|---|---|
| Author | Harzing, Anne-Wil |
| Title | Creating social media profiles. Crafting your career in academia / Anne-Wil Harzing |
| Edition | 1st ed. |
| ISBN | 978-1-7396097-4-0 (paperback, black & white) |
| Subjects | Academic careers, academic publishing, academic development |
| Dewey Number | 650.14 |

# Table of contents

# Introduction

Most academics use some form of social media in their private lives. Personally, I have never been a fan of using social media for personal interactions; I seem to be one of a rapidly vanishing minority who do not have a Facebook, Instagram or TikTok account. In contrast, I have embraced social media in my professional life, and have now used it actively for 7-8 years.

I have also given quite a few presentations at Middlesex and other universities on the "how and why" of using social media to support your academic career. Some of these presentations were recorded and can be watched on my YouTube channel (just search for Harzing social media). I have also run several hands-on "social media clinics" where I discuss the various social media options in detail and help academics to improve their own profiles. The presentations and notes for these clinics formed the basis for a blogpost series and this book.

In this book I will first provide a primer on social media in academia (Chapter 1) and compare the options (Chapter 2). Then I will provide tips for five key social media platforms: Google Scholar Profiles (Chapter 3), LinkedIn (Chapter 4), ResearchGate (Chapter 5), Twitter (Chapter 6), and Blogging (Chapter 7). Chapter 8 recaps the strengths of the five different platforms by considering two key use areas: the use of social media as a source of professional/academic information and the use of social media to share (news about) your research.

Note that this book was written from the perspective of a research-active academic and focuses mostly about sharing (news about) your research. Of the five platforms that I discuss in detail, Google Scholar Profiles and ResearchGate focus mainly on research. However, LinkedIn, Twitter and blogs are also useful to share news about other aspects of your academic job.

I hope this guide will demystify the topic of social media in academia and provide you with the tools to be successful in your social media efforts. I would love to hear from you if you feel this book has helped you; feel free to get in touch with me at anne@harzing.com.

**<u>Note</u>**: This book is an updated and extended collection of my blog-posts on the topic of social media in academia that were published between 2020 and 2022.

# Chapter 1: A primer on Social media in academia

In this first chapter, I will explain the benefits of using social media. They are succinctly summarised in a slide of my recorded Power-Point presentation below.

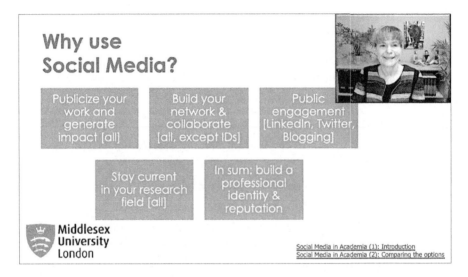

There are at least four key reasons to use social media:

1. to publicize your work and to generate impact, whether that is academic impact or wider societal impact,

2. to build up your academic network and collaborations,

3. to build up your public engagement by interacting with people outside academia,

4. to stay current in your field of research.

In sum, these platforms help you to build a professional *identity* and *reputation*. However, this may still be a little abstract. So, in the next section, I will provide some specific examples.

# Benefits of using social media?

The ESRC offers an excellent guide to social media in academia (see https://www.ukri.org/councils/esrc/impact-toolkit-for-economic-and-social-sciences/how-to-use-social-media/). As they indicate in the guide, social media allows you to:

- promote your research and increase its visibility
- communicate directly and quickly with others who might have an interest in your research
- develop new relationships and build networks
- reach new audiences, both within and outside academia
- seek and give advice and feedback
- generate ideas
- share information and links with other (e.g., journal articles and news items)
- keep up to date with the latest news and developments, and forward it to others instantly
- follow and contribute to discussions on events (e.g., workshops or conferences that you can't get to in person)
- express who you are as a person.

# Why *not* use social media?

Academics also mentioned several reasons to me for not wanting to use social media. They are summarised in the next slide, where I also include recommendations on how to deal with these concerns. First, academics often don't know what to and how to do it. I can completely understand that, but hope this book will resolve at least part of these concerns. And if you are a bit of a technophobe, rest assured that all these platforms make it very easy for you to set up an account. The biggest idiots can – and unfortunately often do – use them, so surely as an academic you are smart enough to figure out what to do!

4

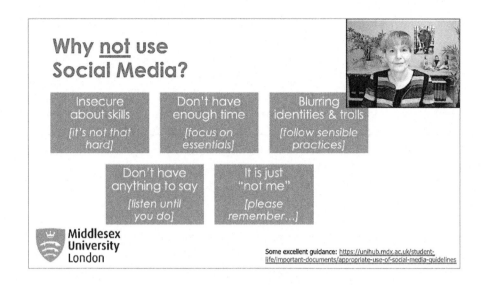

Why **not** use Social Media?

| Insecure about skills | Don't have enough time | Blurring identities & trolls |
| [it's not that hard] | [focus on essentials] | [follow sensible practices] |

| Don't have anything to say | It is just "not me" |
| [listen until you do] | [please remember...] |

Middlesex University London

Some excellent guidance: https://unihub.mdx.ac.uk/student-life/important-documents/appropriate-use-of-social-media-guidelines

I also hear a lot of people say, "I simply don't have enough time". Using social media in a private context, they may have experienced it can be a serious time drain. Again, I empathise. However, I do think it is possible to do this efficiently; to set some time aside once a week or even once a month and just focus on the essentials. In the next chapter, I will give you some tips on how to get the best results if you are time poor.

Other academics are concerned that if they use social media professionally, they end up blurring identities, because they might also be sharing material that's more personal. Again, that's a valid concern, but most of the platforms I discuss are by nature largely professional. Twitter is probably the platform that is most susceptible to blurred identities. So, it might be useful to have a separate private Twitter account. You can open as many Twitter accounts as you want with different handles and different usernames.

Then of course there is the worry of online abuse and trolls. In 8 years of social media use, I am fortunate enough to not have experienced any of this. But I know others who have, and again this is a very valid concern. If you are concerned about this, but don't want to give up on social media altogether there are a few things you can do. First, be selective about the platforms you engage on. You are not going to get abuse on your Google Scholar Profile as it is not interactive. However, abuse is also very uncommon on ResearchGate and LinkedIn.

—

Blogging, whether long-form blogging or micro-blogging such as Twitter, and YouTube videos are a bit more likely to attract nasty people. However, you can simply disable comments on blogs and videos or limit the viewing of your tweets to the people you connect with only. You can also be selective about what you post and decide not to engage in political debates for instance. But if you do research on controversial topics such as identity, anything related to politics, migration, or – in the current UK context – anything related to Brexit or COVID vaccination, you do need to seriously think about whether you want to expose yourself to potential loonies.

Other people say, well I haven't published that much, I'm a junior academic, and I don't have much to say. Fair enough. But remember that you can also just listen to what other people share on LinkedIn, on Twitter, and on their blogs. You can respond to that, and engage and build a profile and possibly followers in that way. You also get to learn what kind of interaction is common on these fora, you get to know the language to use, you pick up the academic etiquette around the do's and don'ts on a particular social media platform. That's much more effective than waiting to publish your first paper, opening all sorts of accounts in a rush, and then either blunder into it, or speak into a void because you don't have any followers yet.

## It is just "not me"

The most frequent concern I hear from academic is something like it's just "not me", without being very articulate about why that is. It is just something they don't feel very comfortable with. It's usually one of two things that they feel uncomfortable about.

First it is having to publicise their own work, they feel it's a bit crash and cringeworthy to do this. Again, fair enough. But remember that publicising your own work does not involve continuous and untargeted aggressive announcements. Publicising your work is simply seeking to ensure that those people who might be interested in your work get to know about it. It's not about boosting your own ego all the time, or constantly thumping your chest saying "oh look at how good I am".

The other concern is usually about networking. In Dutch – my native language – networking was often seen as something a bit dirty. If my parents would talk about networking, they would use it in the context of someone getting something done just through connections, not because they were any good or they had the right qualifications. That's kind of the image I had of networking when I came into the academic world. But networking can also be used in a positive way. It can be used simply to cultivate connections with other academics who share the same interests. And that's the kind of networking we are talking about when engaging with social media.

# "Never cited a paper because I saw a tweet about it..."

Many academics are quite sceptical about using social media, the quote above came from one of my (reluctant) social media workshop participants. But just because *you* don't make use of social media to stay current with your field of research doesn't mean other academics don't. All research on using social media in research communication shows that the more you engage, the more your work is read. And remember, this is not mainly about getting cited, it's about reaching the right audience.

But will sharing your research really lead to increased readership and impact for *you*, either in the form of citations or in terms of Altmetrics or broader societal impact? Well, I guess you won't know until you do a controlled experiment with two almost identical papers of your own, promoting only one through social media. Anecdotally though, I can tell you it made a difference for my own work. Below I provide two examples that get quite close to being controlled experiments.

## Social media use and article downloads & citations

In 2014 I published a paper on trust in multi-lingual teams in a special issue on language in the *Journal of International Business Studies*. One of my co-authors on that paper published another paper in the *same* special issue. I don't think that paper was less interesting or of lower quality, but five years later it had received only just over a quarter of the reads and 30% of the citations that our trust paper did (see below).

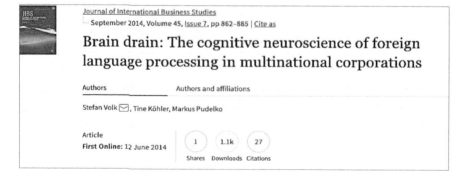

The difference? Helene and engaged in systematic communication about the trust paper through a range of social media channels; the Brain drain paper was left to its own devices. Of course, citations to a paper are a function of many factors, including the quality of the research, the level of interest in the research topic, the timing of the publication, the level of name recognition of the authors, pure luck, and communication through social media.

But given that communication is pretty much the only thing you can influence *after* publication, why not give it a go? And remember that getting your paper under the nose of the right audience doesn't just facilitate citations, it also helps disseminating your research ideas, and gets you in contact with potential co-authors, prospective PhD students, end users of your research, and funding agencies.

## Open access, social media use, and article views

The second example compares the number of times an article has been accessed after 10 days for six articles published in the *same* journal around the *same* time (see below). It demonstrates the powerful combination of Gold Open access – i.e., making the article available free of charge to everyone – and social media use.

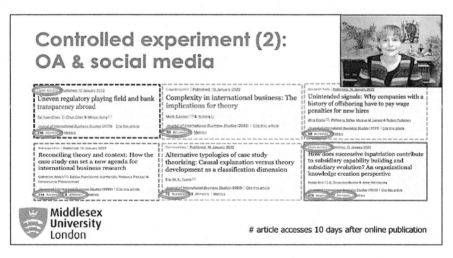

My own article (bottom right), that is both available in Open Access and was shared widely on social media. had an access count of more than 600, three times as much as the other articles that had *either* OA *or* social media sharing and nearly ten times as much as those that had neither.

## In sum

In this first chapter, I explained the benefits of using social media, but also discussed concerns that academics might have about using it. Subsequently, I attempted to convince academics sceptical about the role of social media that it does make a difference in diffusing your research. In the next chapter, we'll have a quick look at the five social media platforms that I consider to be most relevant for academics.

# Chapter 2:
# Comparing the key options

In the next chapters I will discuss Google Scholar Profiles, LinkedIn, ResearchGate, Twitter, and Blogging in detail, with tips on getting the best out of these social media platforms. First, however, let's look at social media use in academia from a slightly broader perspective. What are the key features of these five platforms? How do they allow you to realise the benefits of professional social media use?

## Overview of the key social media options

The table below provides a quick overview of the first four options; blogging is a bit too different to include in my structured comparison. As you can see each of the four platforms has its own unique purpose and strengths (as well as weaknesses). That's why I recommend you use all of them, even if only to a limited extent.

| Feature | GS Profile | LinkedIn | ResearchGate | Twitter |
|---|---|---|---|---|
| Bio | No, but you can add job title, affiliation, keywords | Yes, completely free format of approximately 250 words | Yes, completely free format of approximately 250 words | Yes, only 160 characters, but can "pin" an informative tweet |
| Picture | Yes | Yes | Yes | Yes |
| Customize your profile visually | No, but can clean it up | Yes, add banner image, add relevant sections, flexible text within sections | No, not significantly, but can add projects and feature 5 publications | Yes, add banner image (changed colours, background & font are only visible to you) |
| Display all your pubs | Yes, full list of pubs is automatically generated when you create profile | Yes, but you will need to add them one-by-one | Yes, user-friendly import for most, manual for the rest | No |
| Show your citations | Yes, by far the best option for this | No | Yes, but they are internal RG cites only | No |
| Add full-text of your publications | No, but some/many pubs will have full-text access though GS links | No, but you can add link to a URL with full-text your publications | Yes, ideal venue for this, user-friendly process and frequent prompts | No, but can add link to a URL with full-text your publications in any of your tweets |
| Connect with academics | No, but can show co-authors | Yes, adoption is very wide-spread | Yes, adoption is quite wide-spread | Yes, but adoption is limited in some fields |
| Connect with others | No, not very likely | Yes, you can invite anyone to connect | No, not very likely | Yes, by far the best option for this |
| Follow academics & non-academics | No, though can have alerts for articles/cites for specific academics | Yes, automatic for your connections + manual for anyone else | Yes, automatic for co-authors & those you cite, manual follow for others | Yes, can (un)follow anyone you like with the click of a button |
| Keep up-to-date people & topics | Yes, through alerts for new articles & citations for topics or people | Yes, through timeline and notifications, a bit more focused than ResearchGate | Yes through timeline and notifications, but provides lots of barely relevant info | Yes, through timeline, #hashtags, profiles of people, organizations or journals |
| Share news | No | Yes, through shares, posts and articles | No, but can start a discussion | Yes, very flexibly in various formats |
| Ask questions | No | No, though you can DM connections | Yes, but quality of answers is often low | Yes, public tweets, direct tweets & DM |
| Requires regular maintenance? | None/minimal, periodic clean, add new pubs automatic/by email alert | Minimal, update job changes, check connection requests once a month | Minimal, update with every new pub, check full-text requests once a month | None, you can vary activity flexibly over time, could try to (re)-tweet once a week |

This table is based on my own experience with and knowledge of the different platforms; other users might have different experiences. These platforms are also subject to continuous development. Hence, I do not claim 100% completeness or (continued) accuracy.

## What are the most relevant social media platforms in academia?

There are well over a dozen social media platforms that can be used in a professional context. However, the following five are those that I believe are most relevant to academics. I will discuss each of them in turn in Chapters 3-7.

**Google Scholar Profile**. Not strictly speaking a social media platform as there is no scope for interaction beyond following an academic's updates. However, it is an essential online CV, including all your publications and their citations. For more detail see Chapter 3.

**LinkedIn profile**. Very useful to present your basic CV online and connect with other academics (and non-academics!) and follow their updates. You can also write up news stories and share resources with your own followers. For more detail see Chapter 4.

**ResearchGate**. List your publications (with full text where possible) and define research projects. You can follow other academics, ask questions, and request full-text versions of papers. For more detail see Chapter 5.

**Twitter**. A micro-blogging site and a very useful means to keep up to date with academic news and share your own (and your colleagues') work and achievements. For more detail see Chapter 6.

**Blogging**. A very effective way to diffuse your research to a variety of audiences. If starting your own blog sounds like too much work, you can guest post on other blogs. For more detail see Chapter 7.

# What to do if you have little time?

We are all time poor. However, this is *not* a good reason to opt out of using social media in a professional context altogether. If you do opt out, do this for strategic or personal reasons, not because you think you don't have the time. Setting up and maintaining the key social media profiles summarised above doesn't have to take up a lot of your time. The absolute essentials will only take you a few hours a year and most of it can be done any time, e.g., when waiting for a delayed flight or train ☺.

## The absolute essentials

If you don't "buy into" the use of social media in a professional context, but still want to ensure you have a presence on these platforms, this is what I think you should do.

- Create a **Google Scholar Profile**. Unless you have a common name this literally takes less than five minutes. Many participants in my social media clinics have done this in the time it took me discuss the relevant slide. There is *no excuse* for not doing this. Not having a Google Scholar Profile might be quite damaging for an academic, especially if you are on the job market. I have heard Deans say: s/he doesn't have a GS Profile; I don't believe s/he is a serious academic.

- Set up a **LinkedIn profile** (see screenshot below) If you stick to the basics and have a picture and bio ready this shouldn't take more than 15 minutes. If you want, you can send connection requests to a dozen or so of your key collaborators and co-authors. This can be done within these 15 minutes, as LinkedIn makes sending connection requests as easy as clicking a button.

- Set up a **ResearchGate profile**. If you stick to the basics and have a picture and bio ready this shouldn't take more than 15 minutes either. Most likely, ResearchGate will offer to find your publications. It might not find *all* of them, but if you don't want an empty profile and can't be bothered to systematically add them, this is a quick way to populate your profile.

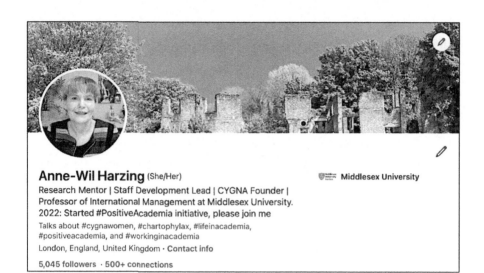

## Maintenance

After you have set up these three profiles. I suggest you check them at least once every three months. If your field is very active on these platforms you might want to check once a month instead, but more often is really not necessary. In most fields, academia doesn't move so fast that an instantaneous response on these platforms is essential. This is what you would do:

- Remove wrongly allocated publications (Google Scholar if set on automatic) or add publications (Google Scholar if set on manual),
- Accept or reject connections requests (LinkedIn),
- Deal with requests for full texts of your papers (ResearchGate),
- Upload new papers on ResearchGate.
  - If it is a journal article, ResearchGate will most likely already have found it and you just need to accept it and add a full-text version of the paper.
  - Alternatively, a more proactive co-author might have already added your paper to ResearchGate with a full text, which means you only need to confirm co-authorship.

## A bit more time? Highly recommended

If you have a bit more time to spare and are willing to do a bit of exploration, here are the four things I would recommend you add to your "social media portfolio".

- Create a **passive Twitter** account (see screenshot below). This shouldn't take more than 15-30 minutes. A passive account only includes your picture, short bio, and possibly a nice background banner. Then create *one* tweet that best describes your interests and pin this to your profile. This could be your latest publication or a retweet of a news story that is central to your research. This means you have a presence, and the account is ready to go if you want to pursue Twitter more actively at a later stage. You might even collect some followers before you do.

**Anne-Wil Harzing**
@AWHarzing

Professor @MiddlesexUni, London | Research & Career Mentor | Founder of #cygnawomen | Provider of the JQL and Publish or Perish: harzing.com/resources

⊙ London, England  &#x1F517; harzing.com  &#x1F4C5; Joined November 2015

**889** Following   **2,620** Followers

- Create a few **Google Scholar email alerts**, e.g., for research topics that you are working on or for a few key authors in your field. If these alerts turn out to be useful, you can always add more of them later. If they are not, it is easy to cancel them. Depending on how well you know what and who you are looking for this might take 10-30 minutes.

- Share an **update about your own research** or your university on **LinkedIn**, e.g., once every month or so when you log in anyway. This can take as little time as 10 seconds if you simply use the LinkedIn share buttons on a publisher's or university's website or 10-20 minutes if you write an update from scratch. We will discuss this in detail in Chapter 4.

- **Review your statistics on ResearchGate** to see how often your work is read, and how often it is recommended. You can also track this over time; this might be quite useful if you are going up for tenure or promotion. For more detail on this, see Chapter 5.

## Nice to have

After engaging with social media at a low intensity for a while, you might develop a taste for it. If that's the case, here are two additional things you can do that can be quite useful.

- Begin **using the passive Twitter account** that you created earlier. Start following some organizations, journals, and academics in your own field and any other fields you might be interested in. Check in weekly to see whether there is anything interesting on your timeline. Share interesting journal or newspaper articles. Reshare tweets that you think are of interest to your followers, or tweets that represent your own research interests if you don't have followers yet. We will discuss the options in Chapter 6.

- Engage in **occasional guest blogging**, maybe once or twice a year. This could be about a new article that you think might be of interest to a wider audience. Or it might be a little research project that is not significant enough to publish, but too interesting to keep in your file drawer. Or it could be a commentary on a news event that has implications for your research. There are several blogs that will accept guest blogs and you can also do this by writing an article on LinkedIn. We will discuss the options in Chapter 7.

# Only if you are really keen

Do you want to become a social media warrior? Has your current professional social media use left you wanting to engage bit more regularly? Here is what you can do:

- **Log in more regularly** to **ResearchGate** and **LinkedIn** to review your timeline and stay up to date with what others are doing. Consider posting or answering questions on ResearchGate or commenting on LinkedIn updates shared by others.

- Use your **Twitter** account more regularly and **"create content"**, i.e., start writing your own tweets instead of just reading and sharing tweets by others. And remember, tweeting is micro-blogging, so it is a good way to practice for longform blogging.

- Engage in **regular guest blogging** or consider setting up your own blog. Before you do the latter, consider whether you will be able to provide content regularly. Although you are not obliged to blog at regular intervals, your blog might not attract much of an audience if you only blog a few times a year. At least once a month is a good frequency to aim for.

# In sum

This chapter presented an overview of the key social media platforms in academia and provided some recommendations on how to engage at different levels of intensity. It showed how much you can do with less than an hour per month to spare.

In the next five chapters I will cover the five key platforms that are most relevant to academics: Google Scholar Profiles (Chapter 3), LinkedIn (Chapter 4), ResearchGate (Chapter 5), Twitter (Chapter 6), and research blogging (Chapter 7).

# Chapter 3:
# Google Scholar Profiles

After a general discussion of social media in academia, the next five chapters will cover the five key platforms that are most relevant to academics: Google Scholar Profiles (Chapter 3), LinkedIn (Chapter 4), ResearchGate (Chapter 5), Twitter (Chapter 6), and research blogging (Chapter 7).

The one thing that every academic, no matter how time-poor, should do is create a Google Scholar Profile. A Google Scholar Profile is a list of all your publications in Google Scholar, including the number of citations to each of them and a visual representation of the development of your citations over time. The screenshot below shows the top part of my profile.

In this chapter, I'll explain why you need a Google Scholar profile, how to create it, keep it up to date, and enrich it. I'll also show you how to get information from your profile through alerts and exports, and how to use Publish or Perish to search in Google Scholar profiles.

# Why do I need a Google Scholar Profile?

Google Scholar Profiles are increasingly used by academics, Deans, and research administrators to get a quick overview of an academic's publications, citations, and research interests.

Google Scholar is the most comprehensive source of publication and citation data for the Social Sciences, Humanities, and Engineering. It includes more publications and citations than the Web of Science and Scopus, which favour the Life and Natural Sciences. An academic in the Social Sciences will on average have 3 to 6 times as many citations in Google Scholar than in the Web of Science.

This is because rather than working with a list of approved journals, Google Scholar simply parses academic publications from what it can find on the web. Hence, any journal publications that can be found on websites with an academic focus will be covered in Google Scholar. Moreover, Google Scholar also includes non-journal type of publications, such as books, book chapters, conference papers, white papers, and even – as you can see in my profile above – software.

## A great solution for "stray" citations

Creating a GS profile is also a great solution for one of the biggest annoyances in citation analysis: the presence of "stray" citations. Note that with the term stray citations I don't mean the existence of multiple versions of the same paper online; Google Scholar normally aggregates those under one master record. Stray citations are records that have not been aggregated under their master record. They typically have only a few citations, and are often the result of misspelling of an author's name, the title of the publication or the journal.

Stray citations tend to be particularly common for "non-traditional" publications, such as software, books, book chapters, and conference papers as there is generally no standardised way to reference them. It is therefore much harder for Google Scholar to figure out whether they do refer to the same publication.

For instance, although Google Scholar does a much better job than the Web of Science to accurately capture citations to my Publish or Perish software programme, there are still many stray citations (see the screenshot below), which – in my GS Profile – I have all merged into the master record.

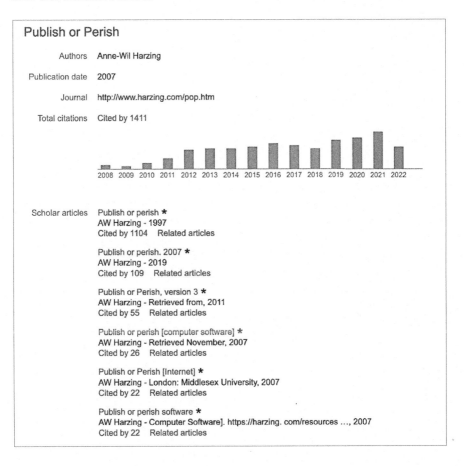

You can merge stray citations by logging into your profile, checking the box in front of the records you want to merge, and clicking merge (see screenshot below). Sorting by publication title will make it easier to find duplicates. Note that the two publications below are separate publications, the first one being a conference paper that preceded the official journal publication. Hence, I have not actually merged them on my profile.

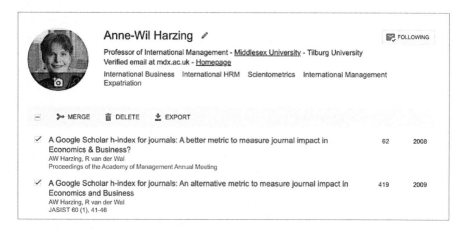

If you have many publications, it might be a lot easier to spot stray citations by using a Google Scholar Profile search in the free Publish or Perish software. You will get a compact overview of your publications and the ability to sort on *all* fields, not just title and year. Below you can see my GS profile in Publish or Perish, with all publications starting with an "A" being visible.

# How to create a Google Scholar Profile?

Creating a profile is very quick and simple. Unless you have a very common name, you should be able to do this in less than 5 minutes.

1. You'll need a Google account before you can begin – use your existing account or create one.

2. Go to https://scholar.google.co.uk and click on 'My profile'

3. Follow the instructions, adding your affiliation information and your University email address. (Remember to validate the email address – you'll receive an email asking you to do this).

4. Add a link to your University home page or your favourite online profile.

5. Add a photo if you want to personalise your profile, which is highly recommended.

6. Click on 'Next step' to create your basic profile.

7. Add your publications – Google will suggest a list and ask you to confirm that they are yours. Look through these carefully and don't import them wholesale because:

   o Publications by other authors may be included in the suggestions if you have a common name.

   o There may be some types of articles that you don't want to include. Google Scholar also indexes content such as newsletters, book reviews, and sometimes even editorial board membership lists.

8. Make your profile public – this means that others will be able to find it and discover your body of work. Otherwise, you will be the only one who is able to see it, which defeats the whole purpose of creating a profile in the first place.

# How do I keep my profile clean?

There are two ways to keep your profile up to date. The easiest way to do this is to use the default settings when setting up your profile. This means Google Scholar automatically adds any publications that its algorithm thinks are yours. So, whenever you have a new publication, Google Scholar will automatically add it. Whilst this may seem a tempting option, it creates two problems: inclusion of rubbish publications and profile pollution.

## Automatic profiles may include rubbish

The Google Scholar algorithm will add anything that carries your name. This includes not only legitimate journal publications, books, chapters, and conference papers, but also "rubbish". Google Scholar draws its information from the web without human intervention. Therefore, it sometimes finds "publications" that are not real. Here are some publications Google Scholar found for me:

Presentation Outline
AW Harzing - 2008

ACOUISITIONS VERSUS GREENFIELD LLLLLL GGGGG LSGGGG LGGGGGGGGS LGGGGG LG GGGLS GGGGGGGLG GGGGGGGGG GG GGGGGLG GGGLLL
AW Harzing - 2002

Rare earth elements (REE) are needed to produce many cutting-edge products, and their depletion is a major concern. In this paper, we identify unique characteristics ...
AW Harzing, W Mijnhardt, Y Ju, SY Sohn - Scientometrics, 2015

The first two are clearly nonsense. The third is a data parsing error. I was accidentally added as an author on a paper in the same issue of a journal in which I *had* published a paper.

For most academics these errors are rare and "rubbish" publications typically don't have any citations. Hence, they don't appear at the top of your profile. However, they still pollute your profile. And if you sort your profile by year some of these rubbish publications might obscure your real academic contributions.

# Automatic profiles lack author disambiguation

Second, the Google Scholar algorithm will add anything it *thinks* you have published. This algorithm works well if – like me – you are the only academic publishing under your last name, or the only one with a specific combination of initial/first name and last name.

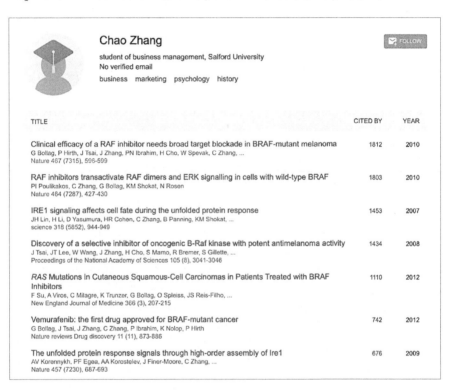

However, this algorithm falls down if you have "namesakes", that is academics with a name that is identical to yours. If you are called Garcia, Johnson, Kim, Lee, Li, Martin, Müller, Patel, Rossi, Sato, Silva, Smith, or Zhang, you are likely to have many academic namesakes.

If you have such a common name, your profile might very quickly look like the above profile by a "student of business management" featuring lots of Science and Life Science articles. This will make it impossible to even find your own publications.

Please note that this problem of namesakes is by no means limited to Google Scholar. Scopus and the Web of Science perform a bit better in author disambiguation as they are using additional criteria such as disciplinary area. However, even their disambiguation is by no means perfect either. For a hilarious illustration of the lack of author disambiguation in the Web of Science, see my blogpost: *"Health Warning: Might Contain Multiple Personalities"*, which found the most cited academics to be amalgamations of thousands of individuals.

## Avoiding profile pollution

It can be hard to keep your online profiles up-to-date and errorfree. At the same time, doing so can be considered an ethical obligation for researchers. Although there might be valid (and not so valid) reasons for *not* creating the various online profiles, once you have created such a profile it is your responsibility to ensure it is accurate and free of errors.

For Google Scholar profiles this means ensuring that the publications listed on your profile are both complete *and* accurate. Just like you wouldn't list non-existent degrees or job experiences on your LinkedIn profile, it is an ethical obligation to ensure that your Google Scholar Profile only lists publications and citations that are yours.

Fortunately, this is trivially easy to do. Simply change Google Scholar's default *automatic* addition of publications to *manual*. This means that you can quickly verify any publications before they are added. It thus prevents profile pollution. Rest assured that this is not a time-consuming chore either. Adding new publications is as simply as clicking on a link in an update email alert from Google Scholar.

To put your profile updates on manual, log in to your Google Scholar profile and Click on the + sign next to TITLE and chose "Configure article updates". Click *"Don't automatically update my profile. Send me email to review and confirm updates"* (see the two screenshots below).

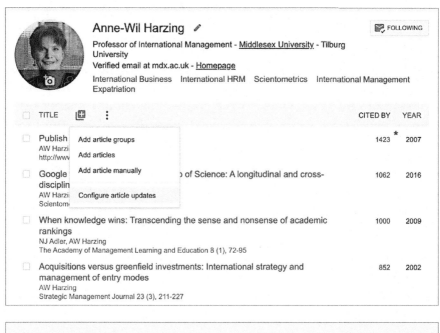

## What if I no longer have access to my GS Profile?

Some academics find that they no longer have access to their Google Scholar Profile. This could happen if a research assistant or research administrator has created the account for you and has disappeared without a trace, or if you created a Google account by using an email address you no longer have access to. In that case, you can write to Google to delete your profile. However, from what I have heard from colleagues in this situation it is rare to get a satisfactory answer to your request.

The next best option seems to be to create an entirely new profile and ensure you keep this profile up-to-date and clean. This obviously runs the risk of profile confusion. However, if your other profile is out-of-date and/or includes several papers from another discipline, most academics will understand what your correct profile is. To make it easier to find your correct profile, you could consider using one of the five allowed discipline labels (see the next section) to say something like "correct profile".

# Enriching your profile

Beyond the addition of a professional picture, there are two ways in which you can enrich your Google Scholar profile: adding co-authors and adding meaningful keywords.

## Adding co-authors

Adding co-authors allows academics to better understand where your research is positioned. You will find an alert to add co-authors in the top-left corner. You can only add co-authors who have created GS Profiles themselves, but it is up to you to decide whether to add all your co-authors or just the ones you really want to feature.

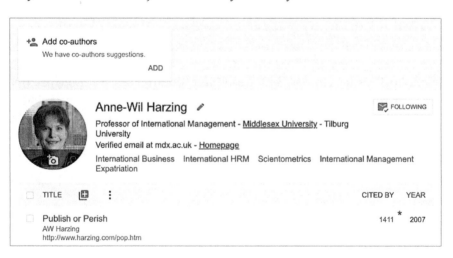

## Adding labels/keywords

You can add up to five labels to your profile. Think of these labels as keywords describing your disciplinary area(s) and research topic(s). Each label can contain multiple words. It is crucial to ensure these labels are meaningful. Labels are meaningful if they represent a *clearly defined* academic community. This means they should neither be too broad (e.g., don't use Social Sciences or Humanities) nor too narrow (e.g., expatriate adjustment, expatriate spouses). Usually, a combination of 2-3 relatively broad keywords and 2-3 more specialised keywords works well.

If you choose labels that are too broad, you will find that there are tens of thousands of academics listed in this area, making it hard for you to stand out. If you choose labels that are too narrow, you might find that you are the only one listed in that area. Whereas this might sound great, most likely it means that nobody will be searching for these keywords. Other academics might also wonder whether your research is too specialised to be of interest to them.

Good labels in the broader field of Business & Management could be sub-disciplines such as: leadership, human resource management, organization theory, strategic management, entrepreneurship, and international business. Finding the right keywords is likely to be an iterative process. First, define some keywords and check whether people with similar keywords include academics who are leaders in your research area. Alternatively, look up some key authors in your field and check which keywords they use.

In my case, I used two relatively broad labels to position myself in my core disciplinary area: International Business and the narrower International Management. As I have conducted research on data sources and metrics to measure research performance, I also added the label Scientometrics. I considered using Bibliometrics, which captures a similar field, but found most key academics in the field used Scientometrics. Finally, I also added two narrower keywords for the sub-discipline of International Management in which I have done most of my work: International HRM and Expatriation.

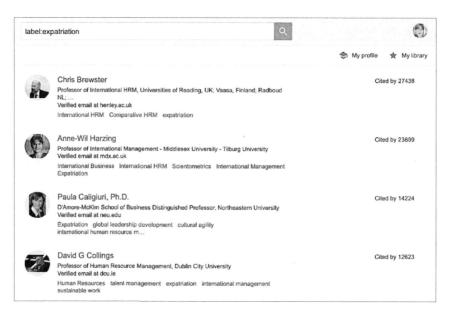

As shown in the screenshot above you will get a list of academics ranked by citations when you click on the label. You will normally be ranked higher within a narrower subdiscipline. For instance, I am ranked second in expatriation and International HRM and seventh in International Management, but only 24th in International Business.

# Getting information from your profile

Once your profile is set up and you have ensured it is complete and error-free, you can start deriving information from it. The two most important information retrieval functions are publication/citation alerts and exporting lists of publication.

## Getting publication and citation alerts

You can use your Google Scholar Profile to keep up to date with citations to your own work as well new publications and citations for key academics in your field. You will get an email a few times a week if your work or that of the academics you are following is cited. You can cancel these alerts any time you want.

To activate citation alerts to your own work, click on the blue Follow button on top right-hand side of your profile (see screenshot below). You can activate email alerts for new articles/citations to your work. The former is useful if you have kept Google Scholar profile updates on automatic. With new article alerts you can easily spot it if Google Scholar has added an inappropriate article to your profile.

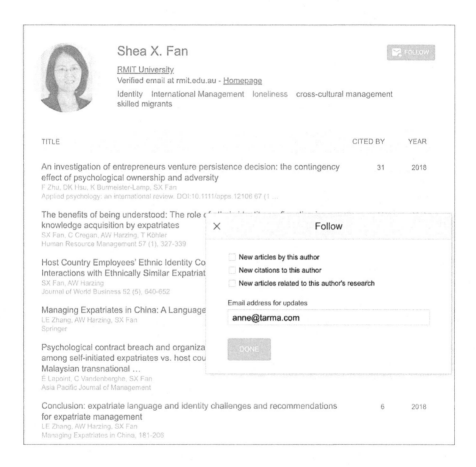

Citation alerts serve a few functions. First, they show you how other academics are building on your work. As such, they also allow easy identification of academics that you may want to approach for collaborative projects. Second, articles citing your own work generally deal with topics you are interested in. Hence, they are a useful way to keep up to date with the literature in your field. Third, seeing other academics cite your work might be a nice ego boost ☺.

You can use the same Follow button to get alerts for *other* academics. This can be useful if you want to keep up to date with publications from a particular author or citations to their work. These could be key authors in your research field, academics you admire, or even your own mentees or colleagues.

## Exporting your publications

If you'd like to have a comprehensive list of your own publications, e.g., for copying into your CV, a website, or a funding application, you can export your publications by clicking on the box to the left of title. This makes the export option visible (see screenshot below).

If you export your publications to BibTex you can also import your full list of publications into your ORCID profile within seconds (you will need to create an ORCID profile first). The screenshot below shows you how to do this. Please note, however, that Google Scholar is not a bibliographic database. This means that it doesn't have complete "meta-data", such as DOI, abstract etc.

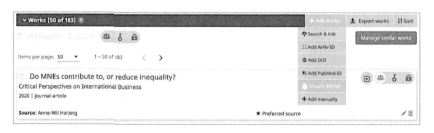

Hence, if (most) of your publications are included in Scopus, linking to your Scopus profile is a better option. You don't need to have a Scopus subscription for this and – unless your name is very common – the profile that Scopus has created automatically for you will usually be correct. Linking to Scopus can be done through the "Search & link" option in the screenshot above. After linking to Scopus, you can always add the remaining publications through Google Scholar.

# GS Profiles and Publish or Perish

My free citation analysis software Publish or Perish allows you to do Google Scholar Profile searches. Thus, any work you put into cleaning up your Google Scholar Profile is well worth the effort as you will be able to display your complete profile with a neat list of publications in Publish or Perish and sort it any way you like.

The latter is more difficult in the web interface, which only allows sorting by title and year and by default only provides you with 20 results. Publish or Perish also provides you with a wealth of citation metrics based on your accurate and complete profile (see top right-hand of the screenshot below).

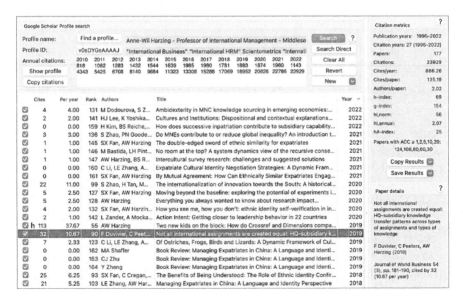

## Searching for authors

The most common reason why academics use a Publish or Perish Google Scholar Profile search is to find their own or someone else's GS Profile. To search for an academic's Google Scholar profile just enter any part of their first or last name and/or their affiliation. Note that a Google Scholar Profile search it is very "forgiving", unlike structured databases which have a restrictive syntax.

For instance, if you can't recall someone's last name, a search with their first name and university might provide a good result. The screenshot below shows a search for anyone with the first name Paul at Middlesex University. However, note that Google Scholar does not place any limitations on what you include and do *not* include in your profile name. Hence, some profiles might not have given names or universities included.

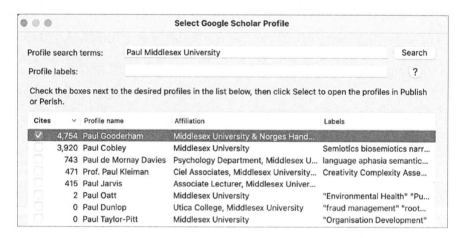

After you have found the Paul you were looking for (in my case Paul Gooderham who works in my School), tick the box in front of their name and click on search. This will show the academic's full citation profile in the Publish or Perish software (see screenshot below).

This will provide a full list of publications that can be filtered and sorted in any way, as well as all relevant citation metrics. Moreover, using the "Copy citations" button will copy your yearly citations to the clipboard for pasting into e.g. Excel for further analysis.

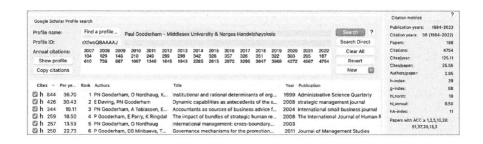

## Searching for labels (key words)

Publish or Perish can also search for labels. This makes it very easy to get an overview of the most cited academics in a particular field. It can be particularly helpful when looking for collaborators, reviewers, keynote speakers etc. The screenshot below shows a search for one of my own labels "International Management". Note that you will need to join words with an underscore. If you don't, Google Scholar will interpret this as two different labels.

Please note that fields in Google Scholar are self-selected and not standardised. For one of my other areas of expertise, I have seen four different variants in use: "International HRM", "International HR" "IHRM", and "International Human Resource Management".

# Searching for institutions

Publish or Perish can also search for institutions. To do so you need to use the "profile search terms" field. This provides an overview of the most cited academics in a particular institution. It might be helpful if you are looking for a collaborator in a specific institution or if you are a PhD student looking for a supervisor in that institution.

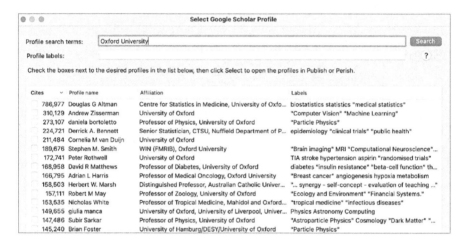

Unlike for the profile labels field, Google Scholar is very liberal in its matching in this field. Hence, if you search for Oxford University it will also match University of Oxford (see screenshot above). You can combine institutional and label searches to narrow down your search (see screenshot below).

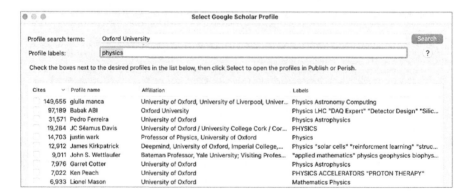

Again, note that these profile labels are self-defined. Hence, there is no guarantee that this search will provide you with *all* academics in Physics working at the University of Oxford. However, it is useful as a first "quick and dirty" approximation.

## In sum

Creating a Google Scholar Profile should be your first priorities if you are working in academia. It only takes 5-10 minutes to create a basic profile. By spending another 20-50 minutes, you can create a "model profile" that includes a clean and complete overview of all your publications, lists your co-authors, and has effective labels that position you in your preferred research area.

You can also use your Google Scholar Profile to get alerts for new publications and citations that are of interest to you and use the export function if you need a complete list of your publications quickly. Finally, using the free Publish or Perish software you can get more out of the Google Scholar Profiles by calculating key citation metrics and searching for labels and institutions.

Note that after setting up a Google Scholar profile, it requires very little maintenance, especially if you put your publication updates to manual. Hence, it is well worth the effort to ensure your Google Scholar Profile is as good as possible.

# Chapter 4: LinkedIn Profile?

For most academics, LinkedIn now appears to be the "go to" place for finding out more about your career history. So, if you don't have a LinkedIn profile yet, creating one should be a priority.

In this chapter, I explain how to make the most of your profile, how to connect with others and recommend them, how to use LinkedIn as a source of professional information, and to leverage it as an effective way to share information and news about your research.

## How to make the most of your profile?

Many academics only include a simple job title on their profile. However, you can use this space to present yourself in whatever way you feel works best for you. Below you can see part of my own LinkedIn profile. It shows my current roles at Middlesex University and the topics that I post about on LinkedIn. It also displays a new initiative that I started in 2022, #PositiveAcademia, which aims to make academia a nicer place for all of us by creating positive microclimates.

**Anne-Wil Harzing** (She/Her)    🛡 **Middlesex University**

Research Mentor | Staff Development Lead | CYGNA Founder | Professor of International Management at Middlesex University. 2022: Started #PositiveAcademia initiative, please join me

Talks about #cygnawomen, #chartophylax, #lifeinacademia, #positiveacademia, and #workinginacademia

London, England, United Kingdom · Contact info

5,045 followers · 500+ connections

If you have limited time or don't think you will use LinkedIn much, you can stick with a basic profile, including just a picture, job title and your most recent affiliation. However, if you have an hour to spare, you can make your profile much more attractive and informative. Note that these additions are "future proof", i.e., you don't need to spend a lot of time to update them.

## Banner image

First include an attractive banner image. The standard blue LinkedIn banner (the bit behind your picture) is rather boring and won't make your profile stand out. So, add your own banner image reflecting what is important to you. For me this is walking in green landscapes and connecting with human and architectural history. Therefore, my banner on LinkedIn and Twitter emphasises this.

In general, nature-inspired banners tend to be very popular, probably because they are inoffensive, and most people find them soothing. However, you could also be a bit more strategic and create a banner that reflects your professional identity. One of my colleagues, Athina Dilmperi, is an expert in wellbeing and her banner neatly reflects this. More generally, creating a word cloud of your academic publications is a great way to create an informative banner.

Dr Athina Dilmperi (She/Her) · 1st
Research Lead Well-being cluster|Co-Convenor PhD Programme|Senior Lecturer in Consumption and Strategy
London, England, United Kingdom · Contact info
500+ connections

Middlesex University

Cranfield School of Management

# About section: your bio

The about section is an important element of your LinkedIn profile. For most academics this is simply your bio; it is similar to what you would include on your staff page or any other academic websites. As you can see below, my own "about" section follows a very standard academic format and focuses on research performance.

---

**About**  ✎

Anne-Wil is Professor of International Management at Middlesex University London, Visiting Professor International Management at Tilburg University, The Netherlands and a Fellow of the Academy of International Business. She is a former Associate Dean Research and PhD Director at the University of Melbourne, Australia. Her research interests include international HRM, expatriate management, HQ-subsidiary relationships, transfer of HRM practices, the role of language in international business, the international research process, and the quality & impact of academic research.

In addition to her substantive research areas, Anne-Wil also has a keen interest in issues relating to journal quality and research performance metrics. In this context she is the editor of the Journal Quality List, the provider of Publish or Perish, a software program that retrieves and analyses academic citations, and the author of "The Publish or Perish Book: Your guide to effective and responsible citation analysis".

Anne-Wil has published or presented more than 170 journal articles, books, book chapters, and conference papers about these topics in journals such as Journal of International Business Studies, Management International Review, Journal of World Business, Journal of Organizational Behaviour, Human Resource Management, Organization Studies, Strategic Management Journal, The Academy of Management Learning & Education, European Journal of Information Systems, Scientometrics, and Journal of the American Society for Information Science and Technology.

As of August 2022, the books and articles listed here have been cited more than 11,000 times in journals listed in the (Social) Science Citation Index and more than 24,000 times in Google Scholar. Anne-Wil has also been listed on Thomson Reuter's Essential Science Indicators top 1% most cited academics in Economics & Business worldwide since 2007 and is in the top-50 most cited academics in Business & Management in Scopus.

---

As I have added a lot of "spice" in other parts of my profile, I prefer to keep this section simple. However, I am the first to acknowledge that it is not very "engaging". So, if you are an early or mid-career academic keen to build up your profile in a particular area, you might want to make it a bit more imaginative.

On the next page you will find the top part of a recently revamped bio by my colleague Athina Dilmperi. Athina is keen to increase her external engagement and work with practitioners and policymakers to ensure her work has real societal impact. This is very important to her, but it also very much reflects the philosophy of our employer. Middlesex University's purpose is to create knowledge and put it into action to develop fairer, healthier, more prosperous, and sustainable societies.

**About**

I am an experienced researcher with a focus on individual and collective well-being in consumption. My career mission is to be involved in projects with significant societal impact, collaborate with organisations and policy makers, publish quality research and deliver high quality teaching.

My current research projects aim to provide solutions to practitioners on how to increase societal welfare. Specifically, I study how particular forms of consumption improve or impair individual or collective well-being. For example, in one of my recent publications, I investigated the impact of dance lessons on productivity and subjective well-being, while my current project is focusing on how inclusive arts can transform communities and achieve community well-being. I have also expertise in the areas of illegal, cultural, conscious and place consumption and on value co-creation. For my research projects, I collaborate with external stakeholders and I am always happy to explore new collaborations or provide consultancy in the areas of well-being, sustainability, inclusivity, place or illegality in a variety of industries or contexts.

Athina followed this section with a more traditional description of her publications and teaching and administrative experience. This way she effectively combined an engaging intro that might appeal to a non-academic audience with her academic credentials.

My research outputs are featured in top quality peer-reviewed journals like Psychology & Marketing, Journal of Business Research, Journal of International Marketing and Annals of Tourism Research.

As a lecturer my expertise lies in the areas of consumption and strategy and I have extensive experience in both undergraduate and graduate teaching, delivering both in-person and in online environments with small or large audiences. I also have significant supervision of master and PhD students.

In my organisation, I have held various positions of responsibility and leadership within the Department of Marketing, Branding and Tourism and the Business School including Programme Leader for the MSc Strategic Marketing, Research Lead of the Individual and Collective Well-being cluster, while currently I have been appointed the Co-Convenor of the PhD Training and Development Programme.

## Career history

Rather than just including your *current* position, make sure you have a complete career history on your LinkedIn profile. Don't bother with your student summer jobs though unless you are very junior. If you wish, you can add detailed information with job descriptions and achievements for each step of your career history.

However, unless your academic roles have been unusual, it is often better to just have job titles. That way colleagues can clearly see your experience and career progression. LinkedIn automatically adds logos for the organizations you have worked for, which makes for an attractive looking list. You can find my own, fairly linear, career history on the next page.

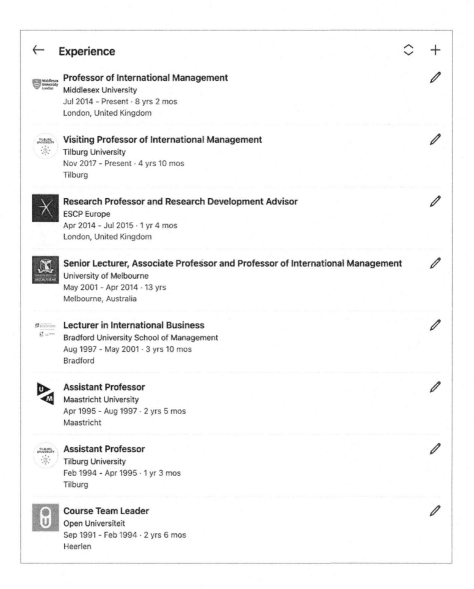

← **Experience**                                                    ◇  +

**Professor of International Management**                            ✎
Middlesex University
Jul 2014 – Present · 8 yrs 2 mos
London, United Kingdom

**Visiting Professor of International Management**                   ✎
Tilburg University
Nov 2017 – Present · 4 yrs 10 mos
Tilburg

**Research Professor and Research Development Advisor**              ✎
ESCP Europe
Apr 2014 – Jul 2015 · 1 yr 4 mos
London, United Kingdom

**Senior Lecturer, Associate Professor and Professor of International Management**  ✎
University of Melbourne
May 2001 – Apr 2014 · 13 yrs
Melbourne, Australia

**Lecturer in International Business**                               ✎
Bradford University School of Management
Aug 1997 – May 2001 · 3 yrs 10 mos
Bradford

**Assistant Professor**                                             ✎
Maastricht University
Apr 1995 – Aug 1997 · 2 yrs 5 mos
Maastricht

**Assistant Professor**                                             ✎
Tilburg University
Feb 1994 – Apr 1995 · 1 yr 3 mos
Tilburg

**Course Team Leader**                                              ✎
Open Universiteit
Sep 1991 – Feb 1994 · 2 yrs 6 mos
Heerlen

## Adding publications

You can also add publications to your profile. To do this just click
Add profile section/Additional/Publications. Presumably, you can
add *all* your publications, but as – like most senior academics – I have
so many I have never tried this. This feature is particularly useful for
junior academics on the job market. They may only have one or a few
publications and really want to showcase them.

That said, even experienced academics may wish to add a few key publications that best represent their research interests. I have added six publications to my profile representing a selection of my recent and older research interests. Below I have included a screenshot of one of my recent practitioner-oriented publications with Shea Fan, one of my former PhD students.

**The double-edged sword of ethnic similarity for expatriates**
Organizational Dynamics · Oct 3, 2020

( Show publication ⬀ )

Identifying employees to represent headquarters (HQ) effectively in overseas units is a management challenge faced by all multinational corporations (MNCs). To date, management of this type of expatriate employees has accorded a central role to culture, such as understanding cultural differences, facilitating cultural adaptation and adjustment, and cultivating cultural intelligence. Although culture is a critical factor in explaining expatriates' experiences, identity offers an alternative angle to reveal the challenges that occur when expatriates interact with host country employees. In this article, we introduce ethnically similar expatriates – a sub-category of expatriates who share an ethnicity with host country employees – to showcase the role of identity, especially the interpersonal dynamics associated with ethnic similarity.

Other authors

You can link to your co-authors' LinkedIn profiles if they are one of your connections, a click on the picture leads to their profile. And if they are not, you might want to invite them, as being a co-author is certainly a good reason to be connected! LinkedIn doesn't allow you to store full texts of papers, the best platform for that is ResearchGate, discussed in Chapter 5. However, LinkedIn's "Show Publication" link leads visitors to the publisher's version of the publication.

# Connecting with others

After sprucing up your profile, you might want to connect with key academics in your field, as well as colleagues in your own institution. To find them, you can search LinkedIn by name, university, or even keyword. Include a short message indicating why you would like to connect, especially if you reach out to people who don't know you.

If you don't care too much about computer security, you can allow LinkedIn to connect to your address book in other applications and automate this process, but I prefer to keep matters in my own hands. Once you have a set of connections, LinkedIn will also suggest others under "people with similar roles", "people you may have worked with", "people in the [geographical] area", and "people in the [...] industry". You can then send an invitation by just clicking on the connect button under their name.

Recently, they also started to offer suggestions for people who are part of the same LinkedIn groups (see later section on LinkedIn groups). Here is an example of WAIB, a group for female academics in International Business, which I am a member of. As I recognised all the names featured on the top row, I did send connection requests to all four women featured here.

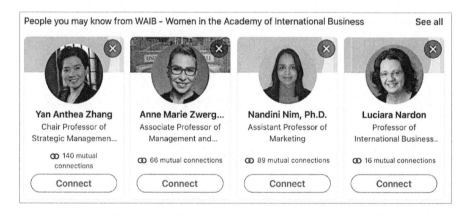

You will also start receiving invitations to connect with others. As the process of sending out connection requests is so easy, you may well receive many invitations from people you have never heard of. This is especially true if you are quite well-known yourself.

Feel free to be selective, you are not obliged to accept every invitation; doing so will result in a large, but unfocused network. It is not rude to decline an invitation from someone you feel you have no connection with. Rest assured; they will not be specifically notified that you have declined their invitation.

# Messaging

LinkedIn has a useful direct messaging function (see the screenshot below). It allows you to message any of your connections directly. It is a little less "invasive" than email and I find it very useful to alert connections to interesting articles or groups.

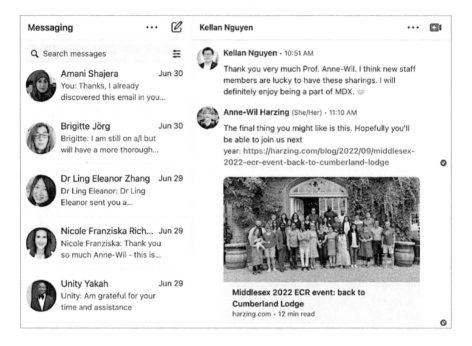

## Keeping up to date with your colleagues

LinkedIn makes it easy to keep informed about your colleagues. It has a special section that indicates recent joiners, colleagues who are promoted or have taken on new roles, and colleagues who celebrated a work anniversary. The screenshot below shows how this works.

As I have a research mentorship and staff development role in a Business School with nearly 300 members of staff, the new joiners section is particularly helpful. It allows me to connect with new colleagues quickly.

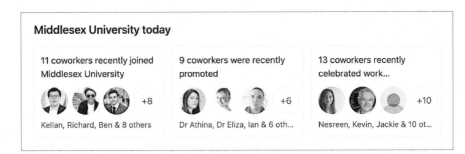

The promotions section allows me to stay up to date with new roles and promotions. For instance, Athina Dilmperi recently took on a new role as co-convener of the PhD programme and Eliza Watt was promoted to Senior Lecturer. Note, however, that if your work for a university, this section will also feature students as your co-workers. Hence, a lot of the news might relate to students rather than your work colleagues. Even so, an occasional glance might be useful.

## Adjust your email notifications settings

I suggest you adjust your preferences to ensure you are not over-whelmed with emails. I have switched off all add tailoring and most emails/notifications. For instance, I really don't feel I need to know about people's birthdays, their work anniversaries, or even my own "connection anniversaries" with them. In contrast, I *am* interested to know if someone in my network has changed jobs. Spend five minutes to make sure the notifications work for you, rather than just cursing all the irrelevant emails you get.

# Recommend your connections

Once you are connected with someone on LinkedIn, there are two ways you can help someone to build up their profile. First, you can recommend your connections for specific skills. LinkedIn will send you prompts to do so, and you only need to click the right button. As most academics will get lots of recommendations for research and teaching (see below) I don't find these terribly helpful.

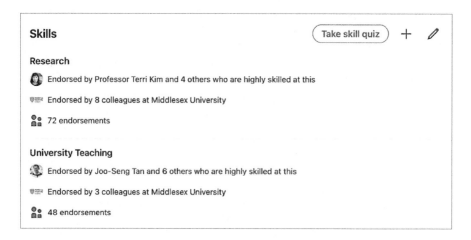

The second, more useful, option is writing a dedicated recommendation for them. This is quite similar to writing a reference for someone, except that it is much shorter and is public. I have done this for quite a few of my connections, including mentees, colleagues, co-authors, or academic service providers such as editors (see screenshot below). For more tips read my blogpost: *"Using LinkedIn recommendations to support others"*.

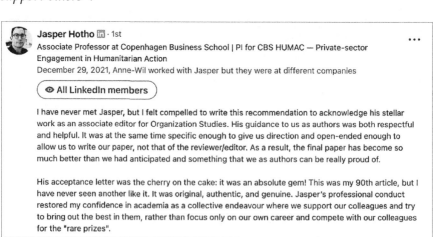

## How to write an effective recommendation?

Having written some sixty of these recommendations to date, I have discovered a few do's and don'ts that might be helpful for you too:

## The do's

- Ensure your recommendation is genuine. This means that you need to focus on what is *unique* to that person. You might well be able to reuse some phrases; I have occasionally. But the bulk of the recommendation needs to be custom written.
- Think about how this recommendation might help someone and how they might use it. Are they going up for promotion soon? Are they looking for a new job? Or is it simply a nice confidence booster for keeping up the great work they are already doing.
- Include positive and unique information ("the hook") early on in your recommendation. Although starting out with how long you have known a person, and in what capacity, might work in the academic world where "reputation by association" is powerful, ensure that positive/unique information is visible without readers having to click on "see more..." (see screenshot below).

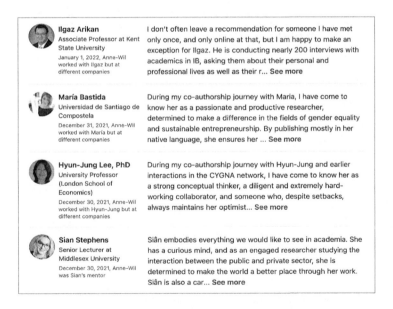

## The don'ts

- Don't write a recommendation for someone if you are struggling to come up with one. The best recommendations are the result of your words flowing naturally when thinking about the person. If they don't, interact with them a bit longer until they do.

- Don't aim for comprehensiveness. It is a recommendation, not a reference letter! Although LinkedIn provide you with up to 3000 characters, I have rarely used more than a third of this. People don't want a potted career history; they want to know what someone is uniquely good at.
- Don't write negative recommendations. This almost goes without saying, doesn't it? It is a recommendation, not a reference letter! You don't *have* to write one. So, if you can't find anything positive to say about a person, just stay silent.

Below are a few more examples that might inspire you to write your own recommendations. Go on and put a smile on a someone's face!

**Helene Tenzer** · 1st
Professor of International Management, LMU Munich School of Management
December 29, 2021, Anne-Wil was Helene's mentor

⊙ All LinkedIn members

When meeting her for the first time nearly 10 years ago, Helene immediately impressed me with her combination of sharp intellect and practical organizational skills, making her the ideal academic collaborator. Our interactions since have only confirmed that first impression over and over again.

Therefore, I am not surprised that she managed to publish numerous papers in the top journals in our field, combining strong conceptual grounding with meticulous qualitative research. In the CYGNA women's network we were all fascinated by her presentation on publishing in top IB journals in which she shared her systematic approach to planning papers from a large-scale qualitative study: https://harzing.com/blog/2018/05/cygna-publishing-in-management-psychology-and-international-business#IB

Most recently Helene has been a tower of support as co-editor in my longstanding IHRM textbook, which will soon celebrate its 30th anniversary. Having almost given up on embarking on new editions, with Helene (and Sebastian Reiche) as co-editors I know the book's future is in safe hands.

**Clarice Santos** · 1st
Senior Lecturer in Leadership & Workforce Management at Middlesex University | Visiting Research Fellow and Member of UNESCO Chair at the University of Lincoln
December 27, 2021, Anne-Wil was senior to Clarice but didn't manage Clarice directly

⊙ All LinkedIn members

Clarice has been my mentee at Middlesex University Business School for the last 1.5 years, but I have known her since she was a PhD student at the University of Melbourne where I was PhD director in the mid-2000s. Clarice is the perfect all-round academic, a passionate and accomplished researcher, an effective and caring teacher who uses her industry experience to good effect, and someone who steps up to any (leadership) challenges with flair and good humour.

Her expertise in diversity and inclusion has been instrumental in building Middlesex's reputation in this area. Clarice has also been an invaluable member of my large female mentee group, her input being as considerate as it is constructive, evidencing her extensive experience and reflective nature. Having Clarice's support makes my role as mentor so much easier!

# LinkedIn as source of professional/academic information

Just like Twitter and ResearchGate, LinkedIn has a timeline with postings (see the next section to find out where these postings are coming from). This can be a very useful source of professional and academic information, but for that to happen, you will need to put it a little bit of work. By default, you are "following" *everyone* you ever connected with, which – if you have more than a few hundred connections – might lead to complete information overload.

Unfortunately, LinkedIn doesn't make it intuitive to change this, but it can be done. Click on "Followers" in the top section of your profile. On the next window click on "Following" and simply un-follow all connections that you are not very interested in. This list is ordered by frequency of posting, so you can quickly reduce the number of posts you see in your timeline. Your connections won't be able to see that you have unfollowed them, so don't worry about offending people.

Follow fresh perspectives    4,529 Following    5,048 Followers

Unfollow to stop seeing their posts in your feed. Don't worry, they won't be notified.

Note that you can follow people even if you are not connected with them. This might be a useful way to keep up to date with academics that have not accepted your connection request. You can also follow organizations that have their own LinkedIn account. For instance, I am following my own university to keep up to date with its news.

Like other social media platforms LinkedIn also tailors your timeline depending on your earlier interactions. If you have liked or commented on someone's posts, you will be likely to see them featuring more prominently in your timeline.

## LinkedIn Groups

You can join groups (incl. journals) and read postings that have been posted specifically in these groups. Below is the LinkedIn group we have created for our CYGNA network.

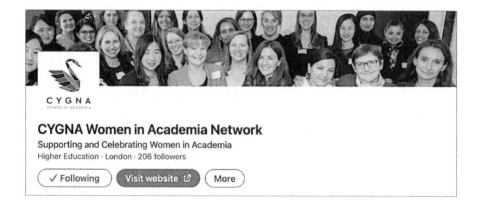

**CYGNA Women in Academia Network**
Supporting and Celebrating Women in Academia
Higher Education · London · 206 followers

✓ Following   Visit website ⬀   More

As a member you can also post information in these groups. This means your posts will get a more targeted audience. However, many groups only have a small number of followers. So, you may get more attention when you post to your own followers. Experiment a little!

## Using #hashtags

You can also follow companies and #hashtags. The latter means that you will see any posts that have this #hashtag in their post. This can be a very useful alternative to Twitter, especially if you don't have a Twitter account or can't be bothered to check it. Please note, however, that LinkedIn's recommended #hashtags are often a lot more generic than Twitter's and you might end up seeing a lot of irrelevant posts.

That said, #hashtags can also be very useful to collate a variety of materials in one place. I am using #PositiveAcademia for all my posts on this topic (see below), #AWHLinkedInRecommendations for all my recommendations (see above) and #cygnawomen for any posts relating to the CYGNA network for female academics.

You can also use #hashtags to collate useful articles for a research project or even for a specific course you are teaching. Given that – unlike Twitter – LinkedIn allows you to edit posts after posting them, you can even add #hashtags retrospectively.

# Sharing news with your followers

LinkedIn can be used to share news & promote your own work. The advantage of LinkedIn is that it allows much longer posts than alternative such as Twitter (Chapter 6). LinkedIn also usually has a more academic audience as most of your connections are likely to be fellow academics. Here are some suggestions of what you can do.

## Sharing with the LinkedIn share button

You can share interesting journal articles, newspaper articles, blogposts or any other material that has a LinkedIn share button. Below left I have shared an article about gender bias in student evaluations that attracted quite a lot of interest. I also share positive news about my university. Below right for instance is the happy announcement of our #1 ranking in research impact in the UK's REF, our 6-7 yearly national research evaluation.

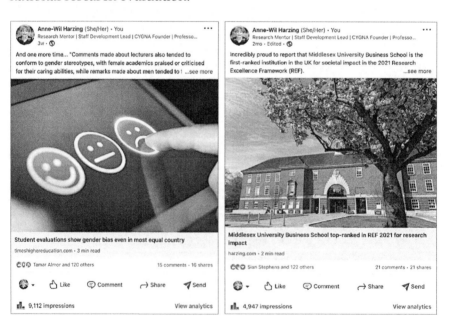

I also share my own blogposts on LinkedIn. Some of these are about research. Below left is a guest post on my blog written by co-author Heejin Kim. It tells the story behind our recent article in *Journal of International Business Studies*. Other posts are about general topics in academia. Below right is a post on disambiguating research impact, which I was invited to write for the SAGE Social Sciences Space.

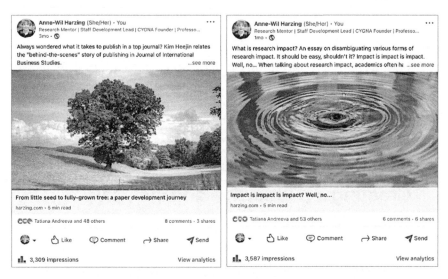

## Direct LinkedIn posts

You can also write a short post *directly* on LinkedIn (refer to the next section for how to do this). You could alert your followers to a recent publication or an event you or your university are organising (see below left). You can even solicit participation in one of your research projects (see below right).

# Writing LinkedIn articles

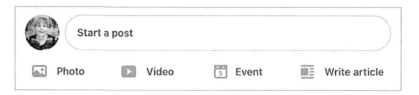

For something a bit more permanent, write your own article. This is a good alternative to blogging on dedicated blogging platforms (see Chapter 7), especially given that on LinkedIn you already have a ready-made audience. You can start writing an article from the same place where you can write a short LinkedIn post (see above). As I have my own blog I write LinkedIn articles very rarely, but I did write one about my work at Middlesex university (see below).

# Featured posts

If you are active on LinkedIn, your posts, some of which might have taken you a lot of time to write, will soon be submerged in a sea of other postings. So, if you would like to showcase some of your posts you can do this in a separate "Featured" section on your profile. Here are two of the six posts that I have featured.

The first is a LinkedIn post in which I told my #thislittlegirlisme story as part of the Inspiring Girls international campaign. At first, I really hesitate to write something so personal on LinkedIn, but it has turned out to be one of my most viewed posts with nearly 37,000 impressions to date, and I have only had positive reactions.

This little girl loved puzzles and wanted to be a detective. This little girl loved learning and reading. She would rather spend time in her own little world than play with others, unless it was playing school with her younger brothers. It wasn't until much later in life that she discovered that s...

438                                                                                    74 comments

The second is a re-share from my own blog. In this blogpost, I talk about all the little steps that *each* of us can take to make academia a kinder place. It shows you how you can change academic culture one email or social media engagement at a time. Read the post for yourself for plenty of examples of how *you* can play a part in this too.

I am sure you have heard it all before. Academia is too competitive. We focus too much on the...

**Changing academic culture: one email at a time...**
harzing.com • 7 min read

66                                                                                    16 comments

# In sum

LinkedIn is an incredibly versatile platform. Many academics only see LinkedIn as a platform where you present a boring career history. However, you can do so much more with it. First, you can make sure your profile looks distinctive, and showcases what is important to you in your academic career.

However, you can also use LinkedIn to connect with others and help them build up their profiles by recommendations. It is also very useful as a source of professional information, and as platform to share news about your research and other aspects of your job to a ready-made audience of connections.

LinkedIn is complementary to your Google Scholar Profile, discussed in Chapter 3, which only lists your articles and their citations. It is also complementary to ResearchGate. The latter is the "go-to" place for sharing your research outputs in full-text and will be discussed in Chapter 5.

# Chapter 5: ResearchGate

Your Google Scholar Profile (Chapter 3) is essentially the publication list of your CV, covering all your publications and their citations. LinkedIn (Chapter 4) is the "go to" place for finding out more about your career history and allows you to easily share your professional news in various formats.

ResearchGate, the topic of this chapter, has become the "go to" place to both store and find full-text versions of academic papers, crucial to disseminate your work more widely. Academia.edu, arXiv.org and SSRN are popular in some disciplines too, but ResearchGate appears to be the most widely used platform overall. As we will discuss in this chapter, you can also use ResearchGate to create projects to showcase your research, keep up to date with what other academics are doing, and evidence the impact of your work.

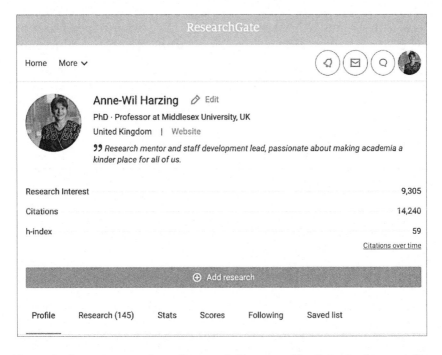

Above is the top part of my ResearchGate profile. It includes a tagline for your profile, and presents various metrics indicating the academic impact of your work.

# Setting up your profile

Creating a profile is simple:

1. Go to researchgate.net

2. Click Join for free or connect with Facebook or LinkedIn

3. Select which type of researcher you are

4. Enter your name, institutional email address, and choose a password

5. To finish creating your account, you will need to click the link in the activation email you receive.

6. Flesh out your account by adding a bio and other CV type items. Make sure you keep it future proof, so you don't need to update these regularly.

Here is my "about me" section, containing a standard academic bio. You can make this more exciting if you want, it really is up to you.

---

**About me**                                                          Edit ✎

**Introduction**

Anne-Wil is Professor of International Management at Middlesex University London, Visiting Professor International Management at Tilburg University, The Netherlands, and a Fellow of the Academy of International Business. She is a former Associate Dean Research and PhD Director at the University of Melbourne, Australia. Her research interests include international HRM, expatriate management, HQ-subsidiary relationships, transfer of HRM practices, the role of language in international business, the international research process, and the quality & impact of academic research. In addition to her substantive research areas, Anne-Wil also has a keen interest in issues relating to journal quality and research performance metrics.

**Disciplines**

Business Administration · Human Resources

**Skills and expertise**

Research Evaluation · International Business Management · Bibliometrics · Cross Cultural Management · Human Resource Management · Linguistics · Expatriation, Repatriation, and Human Migration · International Business · Language · Business Research · Business · English Language · Google Scholar · Articles · Staffing · Cross-Cultural Management · ISI Web of Knowledge · Academic Journals · Citations · H Index · Citation Analysis · Papers · International Management

---

# Adding publications and full-text versions

ResearchGate has an extensive publication database drawn from a variety of sources. Once you have created your profile, it will automatically search for publications under your name. It will notify you of any publication matches. Just review them and accept inclusion if they are yours. If any of your publications are missing, you can easily add them manually.

Here is the top part of my publication list on ResearchGate. As I have quite a lot of publications listed on ResearchGate, you could use the search box at the top of the list if you are looking for my articles on a specific topic.

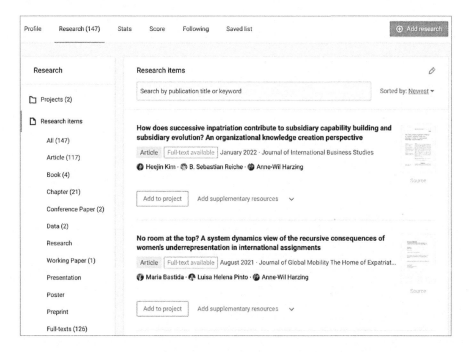

Once you have a complete list of your publications, add your full-text versions for as many of them as possible. The full-text availability will be shown on your profile (see above). If you article is available in Gold Open Access (i.e., accessible for everyone, without subscription) you can upload the official publisher's version as we did for the inpatriation article which is listed at the top of my profile.

Otherwise, simply add the pre-publication version of your article as we did for the "No room at the top?" article shown above. A pre-publication version is the version that was accepted by the journal, but has not yet undergone the journal formatting process. However, your pre-publication version doesn't have to be the ugly "double-spaced, all tables and figures at the back" version you submitted to the journal. You can make it look as nice as you want, as long as it is your own formatting.

You can access more detail for every paper on your profile by clicking on its title. This shows the abstract and any tables and figures that were uploaded separately (see below). ResearchGate also displays the paper's statistics (reads, citations, recommendations), the papers citing it and any related research. Finally, it makes it easy to either share your paper publicly on Twitter or to share it with individual researchers on the ResearchGate platform.

# Creating projects

A little-known, but very useful, function of ResearchGate is its ability to group your uploads into projects. This makes it easier for other academics to understand what you are working on. ResearchGate makes it easy to do this by prompting to you to select articles to add once you have created a project. In these projects you can also add data, PowerPoint slides, or any other resources such as data files. This is very useful if you have a coherent body of research on a particular topic that you want to showcase, or have a new research project that you want to bring under people's attention.

To date, I have not been very active in using this feature. As I have already defined six research programs on my personal website, I just can't be bothered doing something similar on ResearchGate. So, I have only half-heartedly created a few projects. However, one of my former Middlesex colleagues – Lilian Miles – has used it very effectively to summarise her funded work in Malaysia.

Once created, individual project members can add materials to the project (see screenshot on the next page). This is especially useful for conference papers that are less accessible than journal articles. However, you could also use it for funder reports, or even PowerPoint presentations used for project communication. Anything that would help ResearchGate members get excited about this project!

# Project log

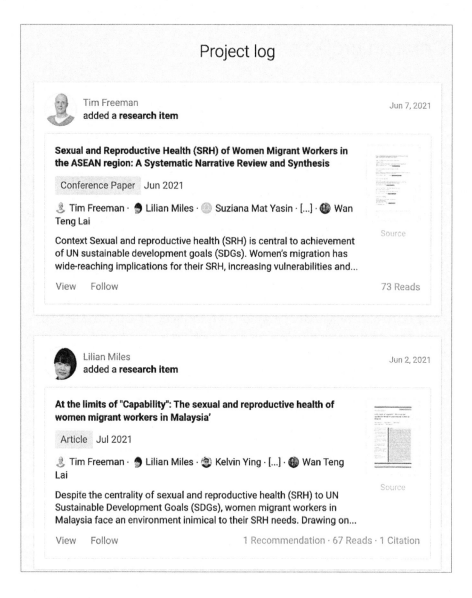

Projects are a potentially very useful feature of ResearchGate. Unfortunately, there do not appear to be that many academics who make serious use of it. Those with funded projects often create a separate website for it. Others simply create a group on LinkedIn or another social media platform or incorporate material in dedicated blogs. As such, finding information about research projects on ResearchGate can be a bit hit and miss.

# ResearchGate as a source of professional/academic information

ResearchGate's potential as a source of professional information is a bit more limited than LinkedIn (or even Twitter and Google Scholar Profiles). Where ResearchGate *is* very useful is in its ability to easily request full-text versions of papers if they are not yet online. Others can do the same for your papers.

Below is a recent paper by one of my former PhD students, Sebastian Reiche. This paper doesn't yet have a full text version available on ResearchGate. However, you can request one simply by clicking on the blue box "Request full-text". This sends a message to the authors, who can then either upload a full-text publicly on ResearchGate or send you a full-text privately, through ResearchGate.

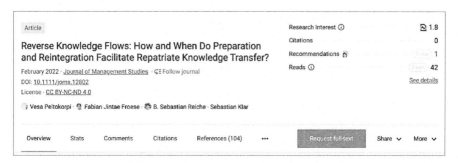

A private full text is particularly useful for those items that you are not allowed to post publicly on ResearchGate, such as book chapters. You can store a full text of these items privately and then send them to academics asking for a copy. Below is an example of a publication where I have done exactly that.

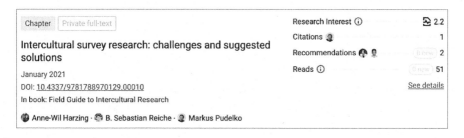

Just like on LinkedIn and Twitter, you can follow other academics on ResearchGate. This might be useful if you are just starting out in a particular field and would like to keep up to date with the work of a few key authors. However, it means you will receive notifications whenever they "do something" on ResearchGate, whether that is adding content, commenting on a paper, asking a question, following a project or a question, or anything else really. This could easily lead to information overload.

ResearchGate also has a timeline, which appears to include not just people you are following, but also co-authors and people who are only linked to you through citations. This might easily result in serious information overload. However, it might be quite useful if are just starting out and are not yet connected to many people.

Finally, you can ask and respond to questions on ResearchGate. However, I typically find the quality of these Q&A exchanges to be relatively low. You are better off going to Academia Stack Exchange or ask one of your colleagues for advice.

## Adjust your email notifications settings

Just like for LinkedIn I suggest you adjust your preferences to ensure you are not overwhelmed with emails. Click on Account/Settings and just spend five minutes to uncheck nearly all your notification settings. If you don't, you might well get several emails a day. As one of my co-authors once said: "ResearchGate's default settings alert you whenever someone in your networks farts" ☺.

If you don't adjust your settings, you will be told if academics engage in any way with any of your papers or your projects. All the metrics listed in the next sections will be emailed to you regularly. Not only does this create serious email clutter, but it also creates an unhealthy obsession with metrics.

All of this might be a bit of fun if you are just starting out, have only one or two papers, and are truly excited with every read or citation. Weren't we all? However, I wouldn't recommend it for established researchers, especially if you want to keep your sanity and get any work done.

—

# Metrics: evidence your impact

ResearchGate provides an extensive set of metrics under the Stats tab. Unfortunately, ResearchGate is not always transparent about how these are calculated. It has also regularly changed both the metrics included and their calculations. They are thus not as reproducible as metrics from data sources such as the Web of Science, Scopus, and Google Scholar. However, they might still give you some interesting insights into the popularity of your body of work, as well as each of your individual articles.

The stats tab provides an overview of your metrics to date, and the increase of these stats in the last week (see screenshot below). By clicking on the "Research Interest" tab – a cumulative metric aggregating reads, citations, and recommendations for all publications – you can see how your own metrics compare to other ResearchGate members. You can even narrow this down to a specific research area as I have done below.

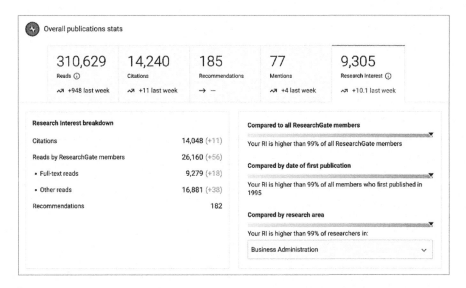

As these stats are private, I can only show you my own statistics. They are not very informative as – being a senior academic with a highly cited body of work – they are in the top 1% of ResearchGate members. By definition, there will be few academics in this position.

However, showing that you are in the top 10% or 25% of academics in your field might be helpful to evidence your academic impact for your performance appraisal or promotion application. That said, I would hesitate to feature anything below that as an achievement as many ResearchGate members might have only a few publications. Hence, one would expect any serious academic beyond the very early career level to be comfortably in the top 50%.

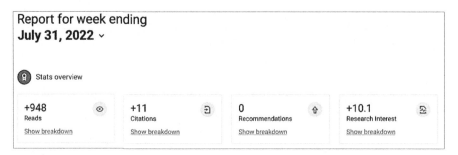

Every week you can also view a report with the number of new reads, recommendations, and citations (see above). This also includes a list of your most-read articles every week, and shows you which academics are downloading or reading your work. You can even find out in which countries, institutions, and disciplines your work is read and cited most.

The sheer amount of these metrics is quite overwhelming, and I think the granularity of them easily leads you to overestimate both their level of accuracy and their importance. However, there is no denying that some of these metrics *can* be useful if you are making your case for tenure and promotion.

## In sum

ResearchGate excels as a "go-to" platform for full texts of academic papers. Most academics now understand how crucial a presence on this platform is to diffuse their research. Its other features – projects, metrics, and Q&As – might be useful for some academics too, but they do come with a bit of caution. There are several other platforms that might be more suitable for this purpose.

In the next chapter, Chapter 6, we'll turn our attention to Twitter, which is quite different from each of the platforms we have discussed to date. It is also a bit of an "acquired taste" for academics. That said, it can be very useful for keeping up to date, and for sharing your research with a broader audience.

# Chapter 6: Twitter

Twitter is different from the other platforms that we discussed so far – Google Scholar Profile, LinkedIn and ResearchGate – in that it doesn't allow you to create an extensive profile. All you can add to your profile is a picture, banner, and a short tagline (see my profile below). Your online presence on Twitter is then created "organically" by material that you tweet and re-tweet.

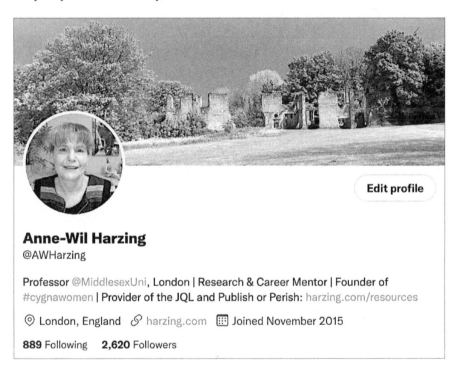

**Edit profile**

**Anne-Wil Harzing**
@AWHarzing

Professor @MiddlesexUni, London | Research & Career Mentor | Founder of #cygnawomen | Provider of the JQL and Publish or Perish: harzing.com/resources

⊙ London, England    𝒮 harzing.com    ▦ Joined November 2015

**889** Following   **2,620** Followers

## How to make the most of your profile?

Twitter doesn't provide you with the option to include a traditional academic bio. However, beyond adding a picture, there is a lot that you can do to ensure your Twitter profile is effective, i.e., clearly communicates your identity as a scholar.

# Twitter handle

Think carefully about your Twitter handle [the bit after the @] as it cannot be changed after you have created your account. As you can see mine is @awharzing. Most academics use some version of their name. A couple of tips:

- Remember that tweets can only have 280 characters, so if your Twitter handle is long, other Twitter users might be less inclined to include it in their posts.

- If your name is common, find a good way to distinguish yourself from your namesakes. One of my co-authors Ling (Eleanor) Zhang shares her last name with thousands of others. Hence, she decided to choose @LingEleanorZ as her Twitter handle.

- Although many academics don't use their titles in everyday communication, it might be a good idea to include it in your name or Twitter handle. Female academics are often taken more seriously on Twitter if they do include their title. Many of my female colleagues have included Dr in their Twitter handle.

# Twitter tagline/bio

Your tagline can be found immediately below your picture and your Twitter handle. Think carefully about your tagline, what is it that you want to communicate? In my tagline I have included my job title and affiliation, but I focus on the three things that are closest to my heart: Developing an inclusive research culture, helping female academics through CYGNA, and providing academic resources such as the Journal Quality List and Publish or Perish.

You can also add your current research interests in your tagline using #hashtags. Another good option is to use your tagline to provide a captivating one-line summary of your "research proposition". I like Ron Fischer's: *"Behavioural scientist fascinated by the big problems in life and how to tackle them"*. Unlike your Twitter handle, your tagline is not set in stone. You can always change it if your research or career emphasis changes.

---

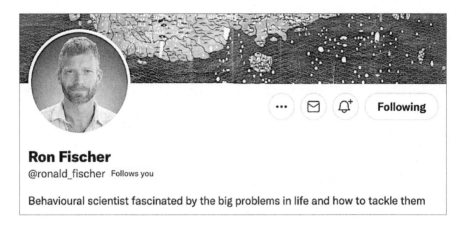

**Ron Fischer**
@ronald_fischer Follows you

Behavioural scientist fascinated by the big problems in life and how to tackle them

Twitter also allows you to add a link to your favourite online profile for more information. As you can see above, I have referred to my personal website as this is my most comprehensive online presence. For most academics this might be their university staff profile, LinkedIn, Google Scholar, or ResearchGate profile.

## Pinned Tweet

Pin your most important tweet to the top of your profile. This could be a tweet about your latest publication, a conference you organise, or a recent achievement. It can be changed at any time. Just click on the three little dots at the top right-hand side of a tweet you would like to highlight and pick "pin to your profile".

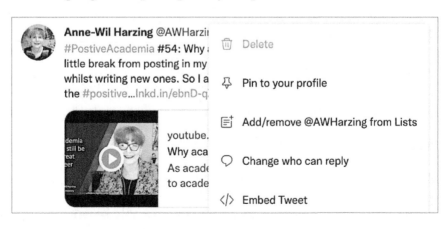

Having a pinned tweet is one of the best ways to turn Twitter into a more informative online profile, as it will tell your followers what it is that defines or distinguishes you. It also avoids your last, possibly irrelevant, tweet heading up your timeline. As you can see below, I pinned a tweet about my role in creating an inclusive and supportive research culture at Middlesex University. It features a nice picture of the ECR event I ran at Cumberland Lodge in July 2022.

**📌 Pinned Tweet**

**Anne-Wil Harzing** @AWHarzing · Jul 27 ···

Thrilled to be back @CumberlandLodge for an @MiddlesexUni ECR event on writing and funding after running three writing bootcamps online. Great to have so many @MDX_BusAndLaw colleagues participating and getting to know each other better.
#PositiveAcademia @MDXbusiness @MDXlaw

## Banner image

Just like LinkedIn, Twitter allows you to upload your own banner image. Pick a nice banner image that reflects your current research interests, your workplace, or maybe a scene from nature. This will make your account memorable and will make it stand out from the blank backgrounds of others.

Walking in green landscapes and connecting with human history are important to me, so my banners on LinkedIn and Twitter emphasise this. Landscape banners are very popular, probably because they are inoffensive, and most people find them soothing.

However, you could also be more strategic and create a banner that reflects your professional identity, possibly using a word cloud. One of my former colleagues researches digital retailing and her banner reflects this.

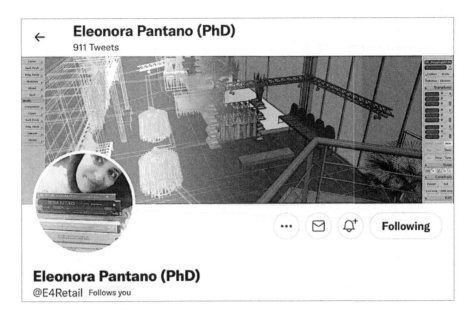

# Twitter as a source of professional/academic information

Twitter can be a very rich source of academic information. However, you will need to invest a bit of time to figure out which individuals or organizations to follow in order to create a timeline that is useful to you. Here are some tips:

- Follow the key journals and organizations in your field. The journals will tweet about issues such as their (calls for) special issues, new articles, and conference workshops where journal editors are present. Professional organizations such as the *Academy of Management* or the *Academy of International Business* might tweet about their conferences, membership news, and interesting books and articles.

75

- Follow key academics in your field to keep up to date with the field. They may also share other useful news and information. In addition to my work in International Business, I dabble in Library and Information Science. I manage to keep up to date with new developments in this field mainly through following Lizzie Gadd, a Research Policy Manager at Loughborough, and Aaron Tay, a research librarian in Singapore.

- Follow the #hashtag for conferences to keep an eye on what is happening in the field. You can do this even, or especially, if you are unable to attend. I follow the Twitter stream of the *Academy of Management* and *Academy of International Business* conferences every year. These hashtags can also be a good place to make a general point related to the theme of the conference. After presenting on the use of metrics in the UK REF at the 2018 Science, Technology, and Innovation indicators in Transition conference I did exactly that, sharing my conference write-up under the #STI18LDN hashtag (see screenshot).

**From insidious competition to supportive research cultures**

Moreover, by using metrics we would all win back the time we waste on evaluating individuals and papers for REF submission, a soul-destroying activity in the first place. Instead, we could spend our "evaluation time" where it really matters, i.e. in reading papers and funding applications of our (junior) colleagues *before* their submission, and in reading their cases for tenure and promotion. More generally, rather than spending such a significant part of our academic lives giving "scores" to people and papers and finding faults in their work, why don't we spend more of our time truly mentoring and developing junior academics. As someone who is performing exactly this role at Middlesex University ⊡ for some 50 junior academics, I can assure you it is also a far more interesting and rewarding job! So from an environment where we all compete against each other to get that elusive 4* hit, let's move to an environment where we support each other to do meaningful research (see also Adler & Harzing, 2009 ⊡ and Return to Meaning: A Social Science with Something to Say ⊡).

And remember, you don't need to be glued to your Twitter account for it to be a useful source of information. You can also simply review the journal's/organization's/academic's profile once a week or even month. And if you don't get "value" out of those you are following, just un-follow them to keep your information stream focused.

# Sharing news with your followers

Twitter can also be used to *share* news about your research. Before you start tweeting, however, think carefully about the image that you want to display. Do you want your Twitter account to remain purely professional, professional with a very occasional personal tweet, or mixed? Think about your audience. A professional audience might not be all that comfortable with tweets about your private life or your cat videos.

Also think very carefully before you retweet or engage with political issues, unless of course you are a Political Scientist, and this is a core part of your identity. Is this something you will still support in a few months' time? More generally, there is no limit to what you can share on Twitter: text, pictures, screenshots, GIFs (static or dynamic digital images), and videos. Any good Twitter guide will give you detailed instructions. Below are a few tips for academic tweeters.

## Tweeting about your articles

If you tweet about your or someone else's articles, include the DOI, so that it is counted in the Altmetrics for this article. I am still a bit doubtful about Altmetrics, but they are getting more important. Most repositories and research management systems will display them prominently. Here is one of my articles that – unexpectedly – got quite a bit of attention as can be seen from its Altmetrics, capturing things such as tweets, blogposts, Mendeley reads and downloads.

Of journal editors and editorial boards: Who are the trailblazers in increasing editorial board gender equality?

Metz, I., Harzing, A-W. & Zyphur, M. J., Oct 2016, In : British Journal of Management. 27, 4, p. 712-726

*Research output: Contribution to journal › Article › Scientific › peer-review*

Below are two examples of how you can tweet about your paper. The first is the publisher image which is automatically drawn in if you include the DOI, the second is simply the first page of the article.

The journal might also tweet about your paper. The two papers above were promoted by the journals in which they appeared: *Organization Studies* and *Journal of International Business Studies*.

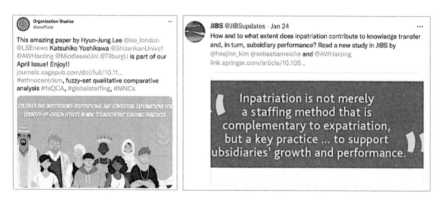

## Make sure you @ people or organizations

Twitter is very ephemeral. Within 10 seconds, your tweet will have been followed by a dozen others on someone's timeline. So, the best way to get exposure for your tweets is to have them retweeted by key journals, organizations, blogs, or individual academics with a large followership (e.g., Writing for Research, Researchwhisperer). You can make this easier by @ the relevant accounts, so they see the tweet in their timeline. However, before you @ accounts, check whether they ever retweet posts. LSE Impact Blog for instance is a very useful Twitter account, but they only tweet about their own blogposts, so adding them just wastes your character count.

## Share news about colleagues too

Don't make every tweet just about *you*. It is not considered "good form" to only tweet about your own papers and achievements. A Twitter (or LinkedIn profile) that is just a big "billboard about you" simply makes you look like a prat.

You can alternate postings about your own work with postings and (re)tweets about topics that might be of interest to your followers or share or comment on work of others that you find interesting. For tips on low-key ways to share your work, see my blogpost: "*How to promote your research achievements without being obnoxious?*"

You could even ask someone to be your "promotion" buddy, where you share/tweet and comment on their work, and they do the same for you. I don't often tweet about colleagues' papers, mainly because I don't always know about them. However, I always try to magnify their own tweets (see below).

 **Anne-Wil Harzing** @AWHarzing · Mar 3     ···
Hi Rima, that's so lovely to thank us publicly. #PositiveAcademia. Have just been presenting at the @CharteredABS course for Research Deans about @MiddlesexUni research support. Glad to see its success confirmed ☺

>  **Dr Rima Saini-Thakor** 🤍 @RimaSaini3105 · Mar 3
> My paper on the racialisation of class & the nation has found a forever home in South Asian Diaspora. Big thanks to @kev_mcdonald for thoughts & morale-boosting on an early iteration, @AWHarzing for comments, guidance & support on a more recent one & @SteveGarner5 for the theory

⟲ **You Retweeted**

 **Lin Zhang** @LinZhang1117 · May 30     ···
Glad to share our new paper with critical questions of APC model: "APC expenses have sharply increased among six countries with different OA policies......Our results lead to a discussion of whether APC is the best way to promote OA".

 link.springer.com
Should open access lead to closed research? The t...
Scientometrics - Open Access (OA) emerged as an important transition in scholarly publishing ...

**Anne-Wil Harzing** @AWHarzing · Mar 1 ···

Yeah... love this paper. A great review about female leadership. And again, it shows how important book collections are in our field.

> **Wab WAIB (Women in the Academy of Int'l Bu...** @Womenin... · Feb 28
>
> #9 on our #Top20 favorite articles list on #globalcareers: Adler & Osland (2016). Women leading globally: what we know, thought we knew, and need to know about leadership in the 21st century. doi.org/10.1108/S1535-... #WAIB's #20th #anniversary #celebration
>
> Show this thread

# Twitter for public engagement

Many academics are mainly followed by other academics and tweet mostly about their own research. However, Twitter is also uniquely suited to communicate with a wider audience. Hence, it is very useful for public engagement, and ensuring that your research has societal impact. Many Middlesex colleagues are active in this sphere. Here is an example by a colleague in the Law School, Joelle Grogan.

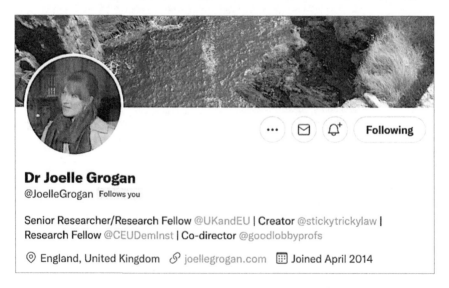

**Dr Joelle Grogan**

@JoelleGrogan Follows you

Senior Researcher/Research Fellow @UKandEU | **Creator** @stickytrickylaw | Research Fellow @CEUDemInst | **Co-director** @goodlobbyprofs

⊙ England, United Kingdom  🔗 joellegrogan.com  🗓 Joined April 2014

In addition to tweeting about her research Joelle is providing simple explanations for complex legal issues with sticky notes. She even created a dedicated Twitter account for this called @StickyTrickyLaw.

*Simple Explanations of Tricky Law in Sticky Notes*

## StickyTrickyLaw

@stickytrickylaw  Follows you

Simple Explanations of Tricky Law in Sticky Notes | Created by @joellegrogan

◎ London, England   ⊘ stickytrickylaw.com   🛗 Joined January 2017

Joelle is also co-director of The Good Lobby Profs, an organization that mobilises academic expertise to counter major rule of law violations, and abuse of power within and across Europe. Their Twitter account is important in communicating their work.

## The Good Lobby Profs

@GoodLobbyProfs

The Good Lobby Profs mobilizes academic expertise to counter major rule of law violations, and abuse of power within and across Europe. @thegoodlobby

◎ Brussels   ⊘ thegoodlobby.eu/thegoodlobbypr...   🛗 Joined March 2021

# In sum

Twitter has a less "academic" feel than your Google Scholar Profile (Chapter 3), LinkedIn (Chapter 4), and ResearchGate (Chapter 5). It also – justifiably – has a bad name for trolling and online abuse. This leads many academics to discard it out of hand.

In this chapter, however, I have tried to show that, when used wisely, Twitter can be an excellent way to keep up to date with academic news and share news about your own research. Twitter is a form of "micro-blogging" and is thus limited in the amount of information it can convey. In the next chapter, Chapter 7, we will therefore look at longform blogging.

# Chapter 7: Blogging

In the previous Chapter, I covered Twitter, which – with its short messages of 280 characters – is a form of micro-blogging. But what if you have something more significant to share that can't be captured in such a short message? Long form blogging is the answer.

I didn't cover blogging in the table in Chapter 2, where I compared the various academic social media platforms, as it is a bit different from the other social media platforms. However, this doesn't mean it is less relevant. Blogging can be a very effective way to diffuse your research to a variety of audiences. There are two blogging options: guest blogging on established blogs or creating your own blog (see below).

## Welcome to my blog!

Introduction to Anne-Wil's blog

Anne-Wil Harzing - Fri 18 Mar 2016 17:00 (updated Fri 3 Jun 2022 08:43)

I know I haven't been an early adopter in the blogging game, but I didn't want to start until I knew I could fully commit to it. Too many blogs dry up to a drizzle of posts after a first active six months! My blog will pull together my 25-year experience of working in academia. Rather than providing mostly personal stories and reflections, my explict intention is to present material that is useful for (junior) academics.

# Guest blogging on established blogs

If you want to try out whether blogging is for you, try guest blogging. This doesn't commit you to writing more than one post and gets you a ready-made audience by contributing to an established blog. There are a range of options: your own or another university's blogging platform, writing articles on LinkedIn, academic blogs such as The Research Whisperer, or even generic blogs such as Medium.

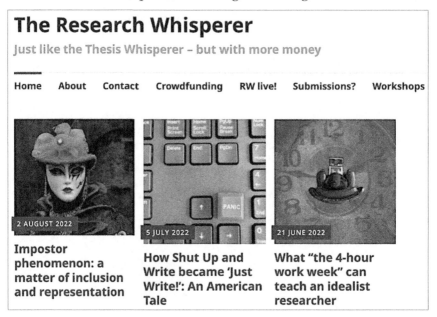

What works best for you is entirely dependent on the topics you want to write about and your own preferences. Remember though that the more generic a blog, the less likely it is that readers will be interested in your specific research or expertise.

## Your university blogging platform

This is one of the easiest ways to get your blogposts on a dedicated blogging platform. It promotes both your own research and your university, so it will make your Head of Department or Dean happy too! Few academics are active bloggers, so your university will be keen to accept your blogpost to keep their blogging platform active.

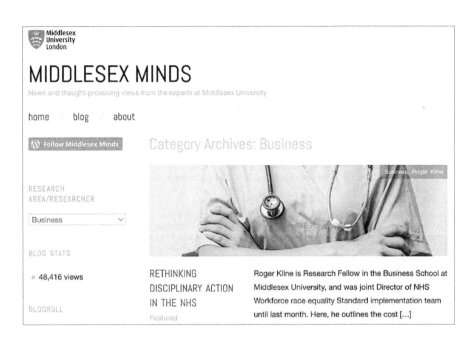

I contributed to Middlesex Minds, Middlesex University's dedicated blogging platform (see above), with posts about my work on creating an inclusive and supportive research culture at Middlesex University Business School and about CYGNA, the academic women's network I co-founded in 2014 (see both below).

March 08 2019

# CYGNA: Supporting Women in Academia

**Anne-Wil Harzing is Professor of International Management at Middlesex University. She's a founding member of CYGNA, a network for women working in academia. Here, Anne-Wil outlines the origins of CYGNA and shares some of the ways they are supporting female academics.**

My interest in the role of gender in academia has a long history. One of the reasons I moved away from my native country – the Netherlands – more than twenty years ago is that I couldn't see myself having a successful academic career there. At the time, I could almost count the number of female professors in Business & Economics on one hand. A 2018 special issue of Economisch Statistische Berichten, in which I co-authored an article Gender Bias and Meritocracy: how to make career advancement in Economics more inclusive, showed

## Other university blogging platforms: LSE blogs

You can also blog on any other university's platform which allows external contributions. The best platform for you depends on both your topic and the country you work in. For Social Science academics in the UK, the London School of Economics blogs are a great option. LSE has a suite of 60 blogs. Some only accept posts by LSE staff or students, but others are open to external contributors too.

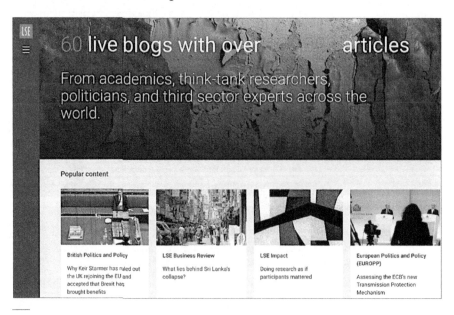

The advantage of posting on one of the LSE blogs rather than on your own university's platform is that – as one of the top universities in the UK and arguably the top-ranked Social Science university – LSE has a strong "brand image" of expertise and credibility. It also has a ready-made audience in your area.

If you are a Political Science researcher or your research has a policy angle, LSE British Politics and Policy or the LSE European Politics and Policy blog might be an option. Researchers in Business could consider LSE Business Review. If you want to write about Brexit, you could contribute to the LSE Brexit blog and if you are keen to review books, but can't find journals in your field that publish book reviews LSE Review of Books is a good option.

Proof over promise: Moving citation metric systems beyond journal impact towards a career impact approach.

Publishing in a high-impact journal carries the implicit promise that the article will also be highly cited. But the proof of this logic remains unsubstantiated. By combining more accurate citation metrics, like the hla-index and the citation-per-author-per-year metric, Anne-Wil Harzing and Wilfred Mijnhardt provide a more substantial alternative to the narrow journal-based metric. This combined metric provides a more reliable comparison between […]

Another LSE blog that I can recommend, both for keeping up to date with what is happening in academia and for guest posts, is the LSE Impact Blog. I have guest blogged on the LSE Impact Blog at least half a dozen times. One was a post about a new research metric, used to create a new ranking of Dutch economists (see above). It was written specially for the LSE blog.

How to keep up to date with the literature but avoid information overload

The sheer number of online services and social media platforms available to academics makes it possible to receive a constant stream of information about newly published research. However, much of this may serve only as a distraction from your research and staying on top of it all can even come to feel like a burden. Anne-Wil Harzing offers some simple […]

Another was a post about strategies to manage information overload (see above) and was reposted from my own blog. The LSE Impact Blog also reposted several of my posts about promotion applications, and about Google Scholar as a data source for the Social Sciences.

## Blogging on LinkedIn

Although not a blogging platform as such, writing articles on LinkedIn is an excellent way to try out blogging. If you already have a LinkedIn account, you can start blogging in seconds by writing an article (see also Chapter 4 on LinkedIn). You can then feature this blogpost in LinkedIn's Featured section to ensure it is widely read by your LinkedIn followers.

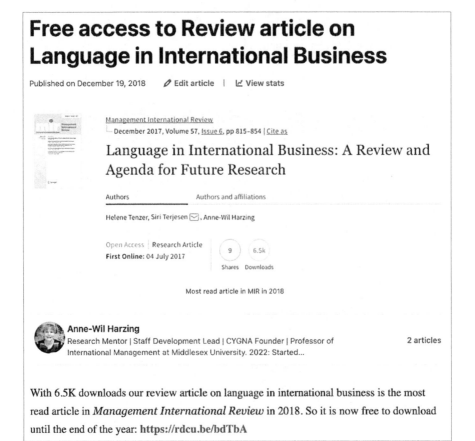

Free access to Review article on Language in International Business

Published on December 19, 2018 · Edit article | View stats

Management International Review
December 2017, Volume 57, Issue 6, pp 815–854 | Cite as

**Language in International Business: A Review and Agenda for Future Research**

Authors · Authors and affiliations

Helene Tenzer, Siri Terjesen ✉, Anne-Wil Harzing

Open Access | Research Article
First Online: 04 July 2017

9 · 6.5k
Shares · Downloads

Most read article in MIR in 2018

**Anne-Wil Harzing**
Research Mentor | Staff Development Lead | CYGNA Founder | Professor of International Management at Middlesex University. 2022: Started...

2 articles

With 6.5K downloads our review article on language in international business is the most read article in *Management International Review* in 2018. So it is now free to download until the end of the year: **https://rdcu.be/bdTbA**

Featuring a blogpost about your most recent research project or your most important academic passion contributes significantly to your professional profile on LinkedIn; it informs viewers "what you stand for". As I have my own blog, I don't write many articles on LinkedIn, but I did post about my work at Middlesex (see Chapter 4) and highlighted one of my papers when it was named most-read article of the year for the journal (see above).

My Middlesex colleague Nico Pizzolato is an active article writer on LinkedIn, writing about his specialty: developing academics to be better writers. Check out his hilarious article on the four ailments about academic writing (see below).

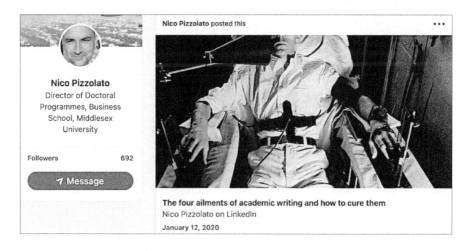

Nico Pizzolato posted this

**Nico Pizzolato**
Director of Doctoral Programmes, Business School, Middlesex University

Followers 692

✈ Message

**The four ailments of academic writing and how to cure them**
Nico Pizzolato on LinkedIn

January 12, 2020

## The Conversation

Another great option for guest blogging is the Conversation, which posts online commentary on a broad range of topics including politics, science, the arts, business, economics, and education. It is a very well-respected platform. Journalists often turn to it for accessible summaries of research, which they subsequently write up for the more traditional newspapers. So, it creates a multiplier effect. However, these days it is quite hard though to get an article accepted in the Conversation. So, if you want to try this, I suggest reaching out to colleagues who have published there before. Below is an article written by one of my Middlesex colleagues in Finance, Suman Lodh.

**Record spend on Christmas advertising as companies try to stem Brexit losses**

Published: December 17, 2018 3.04pm GMT

Authors

Monomita Nandy
Senior lecturer in Accounting and Finance, Brunel University London

Suman Lodh
Senior Lecturer in Finance, Middlesex University

# Your very own blog

If you have acquired a taste for blogging, find the LinkedIn article format too constraining, don't have a university blogging platform, have discovered that generic platforms like Medium drown your posts in thousands of others, or you simply don't want to depend on acceptance from blogs run by other universities or organizations, you could consider setting up your own blog.

This provides you with the largest amount of flexibility to manage your own content. For my own blog on Harzing.com, I use a content management system that was custom designed for me, and which integrates with the rest of my website. There are, however, plenty of free solutions – such as Blogger and Wordpress – that allow you to start blogging straight away.

I started blogging in March 2016 and have now clocked up more than 350 postings. Although my first posts took 6-8 hours to write, these days I can often create a post in a few hours, or much less if it is a simple report on a seminar or new article. You do not need to post weekly, like I do, but committing to regular new posts, ideally at least monthly, does help to build up an audience for your blog.

---

# What can you blog about?

Pretty much anything! To get a regular audience, however, it helps if your blog has a coherent theme and purpose. My main purpose in starting my blog was a desire to share my experience in academia with junior academics and/or inexperienced researchers, especially those who don't have senior colleagues that they can ask for advice. Hence many of my posts are in the categories Academia Behind the Scenes and Academic Etiquette. Here are two examples:

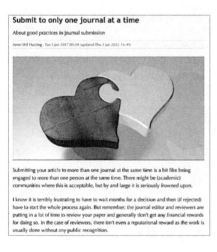

**Submit to only one journal at a time**

About good practices in journal submission

Anne-Wil Harzing · Tue 3 Jun 2017 09:39 (updated Thu 2 Jun 2022 16:49)

Submitting your article to more than one journal at the same time is a bit like being engaged to more than one person at the same time. There might be (academic) communities where this is acceptable, but by and large it is seriously frowned upon.

I know it is terribly frustrating to have to wait months for a decision and then (if rejected) have to start the whole process again. But remember: the journal editor and reviewers are putting in a lot of time to review your paper and generally don't get any financial rewards for doing so. In the case of reviewers, there isn't even a reputational reward as the work is usually done without any public recognition.

**What is that conference networking thing all about?**

Reflections on the importance of networking in academia and tips on how to do it

Anne-Wil Harzing · Wed 1 Nov 2017 08:11 (updated Thu 2 Jun 2022 14:33)

If you are anything like me, your initial association with the word networking will be negative. When I grew up in the Netherlands it was almost a "dirty" word and it seems I am not the only one who has this association ⇗. It implied that you got to where you were only because of your contacts, not because of any inherent skills, education, or good performance. This certainly was a big part of my initial reluctance to engage in academic networking.

However, after a while I did start to see that academia is no different from "real life" in this respect. Just like "normal people" academics prefer to work with people they know and trust. Just like "normal consumers" they will also pay more attention to products (read publications) or recommendations (read references) from brands (read journals and universities) and people (read other academics) they know and trust.

I also use my blog to provide support for Publish or Perish, the free software for citation analysis that I have offered since 2006, and to introduce fellow academics to my own research (see below).

**The changing usage of Publish or Perish over the years: where, why, when, what & who?**

Celebrating 15 years of Publish or Perish with an analysis of its usage over the years

Anne-Wil Harzing · Tue 26 Jan 2021 13:25 updated Thu 2 Jun 2022 12:20)

This year Publish or Perish ⇗ is celebrating its 15th anniversary. So I thought it would be nice to look back to where, why, when, and by whom it has been used over the years, and what they would have used if PoP hadn't been around. There has been quite a bit of change over the years, although the PoP features that users like most have remained quite stable. Here is a word-cloud from the user survey I have been running since 2015 ⇗ (please complete it if you haven't yet!).

**Beyond expatriation: How inpatriation supports subsidiary growth and performance**

Telling the story of the background, motivation, and key findings of our study on inpatriation, subsidiary growth and performance

Heejin Kim · Mon 25 Apr 2022 20:11 (updated Wed 27 Apr 2022 18:02)

'Mobility of individuals' is a powerful mechanism for facilitating knowledge transfer in MNCs, and expatriation has featured prominently in this discussion. More recently, as scholars have turned their attention to the diversification of global work arrangements, inpatriation (the international assignment of employees from an MNC's foreign subsidiary to its headquarters) has received increasing attention.

Moreover, I report on conferences I have visited or seminars I have given at other universities, and have a "classic papers" section, with articles that I consider to be particularly impactful.

**Language & HRD: Keynote at Taipei AHRD conference**

Reports on my week-long visit to Taiwan in 2013, the closest I ever came to being a VIP

Anne-Wil Harzing · Sat 28 Nov 2020 14:38 updated Thu 2 Jun 2022 12:28)

In November 2013, a long time before I started my blog, I spent a week in Taipei at the invitation of Chun Shin Limited - ETS TOEIC Country Master Distributor to share my research on language in international business ✎. It was my last international trip from Australia and the closest I ever came to feeling like a VIP: business class flights, a hotel room bigger than most Taiwanese apartments, and lots of wonderful meetings, lunches and dinners. Of all my international trips I have the most enduring memories of this once, so I decided to write up my visit restrospectively.

**Wives of the organization - 30 years on...**

Celebrating International Women's day with a reprint of a post on Anne Huff's classic treatise that has lost none of its potency

Anne-Wil Harzing · Mon 8 Mar 2021 07:31 (updated Tue 19 Apr 2022 09:24)

In celebration of International Women's day tomorrow I am reposting my 2016 blogpost on Anne Huff's "Wives of the organization". As a young academic in the early 1990s I received a copy of Anne Huff's ✎ "Wives of the organization", which describes how gendered interactions in the workplace may subvert success for female academics. And with "copy" I do mean an actual paper copy that was grey from being photocopied again and again! Remember "the Web" didn't really exist back then and few people even regularly used email. Heck, it was only a few years earlier that I still did my university assignments on a typewriter.

Inspiration for my posts comes from my daily academic life. Whenever I provide substantive advice to Middlesex colleagues, CYGNA members or other academics, I consider writing it up as a blogpost so that it can benefit a wider audience. This also provides me with a ready-to-use stock of posts that I can refer to whenever someone asks me about a particular topic. So, rather than typing up similar advice to dozens of academics or maintaining email templates, I can simply refer them to the blogpost in question. I have found this to be a great time-saver; it is the only way I can continue to help other academics without it taking up all my time.

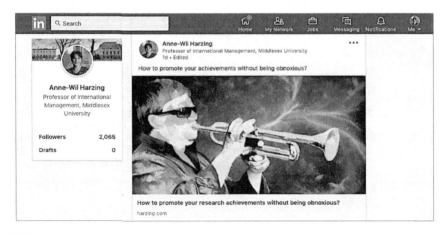

Where possible I also try to turn frustrations into more constructive blogposts. After mounting irritation with colleagues who seem to put their entire CV in their email signature, I wrote the above blogpost. Its popularity whenever I share it on LinkedIn suggests I am not the only one being frustrated with this practice ☺.

## Writing about a stream of research

I have also written quite a few blogposts about a stream of research streams, rather than individual articles. For instance, I have studied cross-country differences in response styles in mail surveys, a topic that was not widely known in International Business. So, I wrote up my studies on this, and also referred to some related methodological articles in international business (see bottom left).

As such, the post would be useful for scholars doing survey research in international business. As survey responses also differ depending on whether questionnaires are distributed in someone's native language or in English, I wrote up another blogpost on my stream of research on this (see bottom right).

**What if fully agree doesn't mean the same thing across cultures?**

Explains how response style difference between countries can distort cross-national comparisons

Anne-Wil Harzing - Thu 2 Feb 2017 08:55 (updated Sun 24 Apr 2022 10:55)

Studies of attitudes across countries generally rely on a comparison of aggregated mean scores to Likert-scale questions. This presupposes that when people complete a questionnaire, their answers are based on the substantive meaning of the items to which they respond. However, people's responses are also influenced by their response style. Hence, the studies we conduct might simply reflect differences in the way people respond to surveys, rather than picking up real differences in phenomena across countries.

**Language effects in international mail surveys**

Explains how questionnaire language might influence the responses received in cross-cultural research

Anne-Wil Harzing - Sun 10 Jun 2018 09:10 (updated Sun 24 Apr 2022 10:53)

Languages have always fascinated me, right from the days of my teens when I studied six languages at secondary school (Dutch, English, French, German, Latin and Greek). I graduated in five of them, adding only Geography and History to my selection and taking Economics as a supplementary. It was what was – and apparently still is – in rather derogatory terms called a "pretpakket ☺", i.e. the "easy" option, taken only by pupils who have no ability in Science subjects.

I have also done a lot of research on rankings, be it journal rankings, university rankings, or rankings of academics, and researched the data sources and metrics used in these rankings. So, again, I wrote up a post summarising nine articles on this topic (see below left).

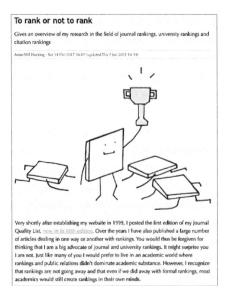

Doing a post like this works very well if you are not just wanting to share your *past* research but also do *further* research. One of my co-authors, Helene Tenzer, does research on multilingual teams (see above right). She has published a couple of articles on different elements of multilingual teamwork and has briefly summarised each of them in the post. She has used this blogpost to go to companies.

All her work is interview-based. So, to go to companies and say "this is the work I have been doing" is very useful. They are going to more likely to read this blogpost than her academic articles. With this she can give a quick introduction about her research, and companies can see she has a very credible profile in this field. So, they are more likely to let her in and give her a chance to interview their staff.

## Video blogposts

During the pandemic, I have really taken to creating videos. I even opened my own YouTube channel: Harzing Academic Resources (see below). Although most of my videos relate to my mentoring and staff development work, you could create videos about your own research too. In fact, these days there are quite a few journals that offer you the opportunity to do so.

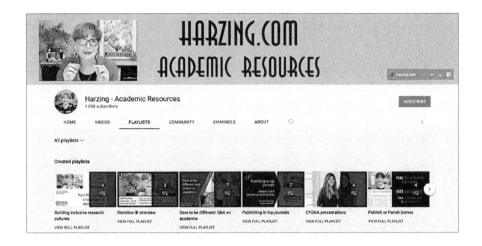

However, what I want to draw your attention to is the combination of videos and blogposts. YouTube makes it very easy to embed your videos into any website. Below are two examples of blogposts that cover interviews I did, one with the *The Academic Woman Magazine* with Anatu Mahama and the other in the *IB Frontline* series with Il-gaz Arikan. Both relate to my work in research mentoring.

Combining your own or the journal's YouTube videos with blog-posts gives your research and external engagement maximum exposure. For more recommendations on how to effectively combine various social media see Chapter 8: Putting it all together.

---

# Harzing.com guest blogging

As my blog has become widely read, I have also started featuring guest posts. Guest posts add variety to a blog, and give the main blogger [me!] a break from regular blogging. Many Middlesex colleagues looking for a wider audience have used this opportunity. Read for instance: *"Own your place in the world by writing a book"* by Nico Pizzolato, and *"R&D Internationalization to China: MNEs' new favourite destination"* by Shasha Zhao.

Members of CYGNA – the support network for female academics that I co-founded in 2014 – also post about their own research on my blog, see for instance *"Mobility and gender matter in speed of promotion and development of career capital"* or *"Publier or perir": English in French academia"*. Some are even posting about their staff or student development work. Below are two of Tatiana Andreeva's excellent – and very popular – posts about literature reviews.

**Want to publish a literature review? Think of it as an empirical paper**

What to consider if you want to publish a literature review paper

Tatiana Andreeva - Fri 23 Apr 2021 07:50 (updated Thu 2 Jun 2022 12:13)

*[Guest post by CYGNA member Tatiana Andreeva]*

When you've been reading a lot on a particular topic – for example, reviewing the literature for your research project or for your PhD – at some point it looks like you have enough material and reflections to publish this piece of work as a separate paper. Recognize this? If you ever tried it, you might know that publishing a literature review paper in an academic journal is a tricky task. The literature review publications come in so many forms, and there is no single cheat-sheet or established format like for empirical papers that you could follow to ensure success in publication.

Through my own journey of trial-and-error on this path, as well as through reviewing for journals and for PhD students in my course, I came up with an idea that will help you to increase the chances of publishing a literature review: think of a literature review as simply another empirical research project. Think of it as an empirical study, in which your data comes not from your usual fieldwork but from the articles that you review.

**Do you really want to publish your literature review? Advice for PhD students**

Why publishing your literature review as your first paper may not be a good idea

Tatiana Andreeva - Sun 20 Jun 2021 08:20 (updated Thu 2 Jun 2022 12:09)

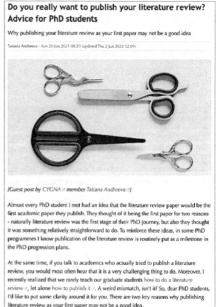

*[Guest post by CYGNA member Tatiana Andreeva]*

Almost every PhD student I met had an idea that the literature review paper would be the first academic paper they publish. They thought of it being the first paper for two reasons – naturally literature review was the first stage of their PhD journey, but also they thought it was something relatively straightforward to do. To reinforce these ideas, in some PhD programmes I know publication of the literature review is routinely put as a milestone in the PhD progression plans.

At the same time, if you talk to academics who actually tried to publish a literature review, you would most often hear that it is a very challenging thing to do. Moreover, I recently realized that we rarely teach our graduate students how to do a literature review, let alone how to publish it. A weird mismatch, isn't it? So, dear PhD students, I'd like to put some clarity around it for you. There are two key reasons why publishing literature review as your first paper may not be a good idea.

Finally, Christa Sathish has guest published a wonderful series of posts on my blog on the topic of her PhD – professional social media use in academia – focusing on the role of care. Do check them out!

# In sum

Blogging is a great way to bring your research under the attention of a lay audience. Increasingly though, even academics prefer short and easily digestible summaries of your research before committing to read the entire article. Hence your blogging is likely to reach both an academic and a non-academic audience.

There are plenty of opportunities to guest blog, so I suggest you give it a try. You might well find you acquire a taste for blogging. I find the immediacy and much freer writing style a welcome antidote to the long timelines and often constrained writing style of academic journal articles.

# Chapter 8: Putting it all together

In the previous seven chapters, I provided a general introduction to using social media in academia (Chapter 1), compared key options (Chapter 2), and provided tips for five key social media platforms: Google Scholar Profiles (Chapter 3), LinkedIn (Chapter 4), Research-Gate (Chapter 5), Twitter (Chapter 6), and Blogging (Chapter 7).

This final chapter recaps the strengths of the five different platforms by considering two key use areas: the use of social media as a source of professional/academic information and the use of social media to share (news about) your research. Finally, it shows how the various platforms can be used to reinforce each other when sharing news about your research.

## Social media as a source of professional/academic information

As I explained in the five chapters about Google Scholar Profiles, LinkedIn, ResearchGate, Twitter, and Blogging these social media platforms can be a useful source of professional/academic information. That is provided you are willing to spend a bit of time setting them up in a way that works for you. Each of these five social media platforms has their own strengths.

### Google Scholar Citation alerts: absolutely essential

As I explained in my chapter about Google Scholar Profiles, you can create email alerts for citations to your own and others' work, as well as alerts for new articles by specific academics. Although not part of the Google Scholar Profiles themselves, when you log in to your Google Scholar Profile, you can also set up alerts about specific *topics* in Google Scholar.

As Google Scholar is the most comprehensive source of academic publications, these alerts provide you with an excellent way to keep informed about interesting work in your areas of interest without *any* effort on your part. You can also add, change, or cancel alerts any time. In fact, a link to cancel your alert is included in every email alert.

I have found Google Scholar email alerts to be incredibly useful. The screenshot below shows a recent alert with two articles citing my own work. The first article is of interest to me because of its focus on the role of distance in International Business, a topic on which I have published several articles (see my blogpost *"Should we distance ourselves from the cultural distance concept?"*).

---

**Cross-national distance and international business: an analysis of the most influential recent models**

C López-Duarte, MM Vidal-Suárez, B González-Díaz - Scientometrics, 2019

Cross-national distance among countries has been of central interest in International Business and Management research. Therefore, different efforts have been made to develop models/measurements to address this issue. In this article we identify the ...

**Konflikte in internationalen Unternehmen: Vielfalt, Widersprüche und Paradoxien interkultureller Kommunikation**

AS Wagner - 2019

Die Mixed-Methods-Studie von Ariane-Sissy Wagner untersucht Konflikte, die in der Teamarbeit global agierender Unternehmen entstehen. Dabei bezieht sich die Autorin auf interkulturelle interpersonale Kommunikationskonflikte. Der Ansatz ist ...

---

However, without a Google Scholar alert most International Business scholars would have been unlikely to stumble upon this article as it was published in a bibliometrics journal. And even though I *do* read *Scientometrics* myself – I do some research in the field of bibliometrics – without a Google Scholar alert I wouldn't have found this particular article until I did my 3-monthly review of journals.

The second article is a very useful German book dealing with intercultural communication, an area in which I have just started a new research project. It is a book from a publisher that I do not receive any publicity from. Hence, without the Google Scholar alert I would most likely have never found it.

# LinkedIn and ResearchGate:
## good for specific purposes

LinkedIn and ResearchGate do not feature highly in my "keeping informed on recent research" strategy, but I do look at what people in my network share on LinkedIn. Here are two COVID-19 related publications by two of my talented *and* social media active mentees: Helene Tenzer and Shasha Zhao. It is unlikely that I would have spotted these publications without their respective LinkedIn posts.

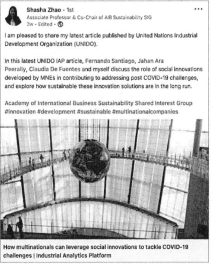

These two social media platforms also have their own specific, more narrowly focused, purposes. LinkedIn is a good way to keep up to date with job moves and/or promotions of people in my academic network; I like to be able to congratulate my academic friends on these achievements as they are so rare in our profession (see also my book on *Writing Effective Promotion Applications* (2022) in the same Working in Academia series).

As discussed in Chapter 5 on ResearchGate, I do not find its social media timeline very effective. However, ResearchGate is my "go-to place" to source or request full-text papers of articles that I cannot access through my university library. These days I rarely need to write to authors to request a reprint.

# Twitter: more useful than you might think

The platform that surprised me most was Twitter. I have lost count of the number of times I have found an interesting publication – whether academic or non-academic – on Twitter. I have also learned about forthcoming special issues of journals and about interesting workshops I didn't know about. Heck, I even got the news that I had won a major award through Twitter (see below).

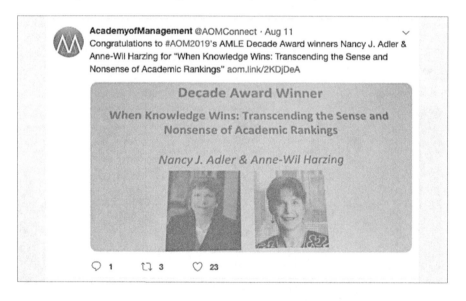

Would I have received most of this information through other channels anyway? Quite possibly, but not in all cases. Moreover, it would likely have been weeks or months after hearing about it on Twitter.

I have also found Twitter a surprisingly effective way to find out what colleagues in my own institution are doing, provided they have an account of course. I promise you; you'll discover that many of your colleagues have hidden depths.

Given that part of my role at Middlesex is to connect colleagues with each other as well as with my external networks, Twitter accounts are very useful; there is only so much you can learn from a staff page or other social media profiles. Twitter is often a very good way to find out "what makes someone tick".

Of course, it works the other way around too. Colleagues can see you presenting at a conference or even proudly receiving an award. With most academics feeling that they are more appreciated *outside* their own institution than within, a bit of visibility of what you are up to won't hurt. I am not suggesting going on a blatant "self-branding" exercise (remember "How to promote your research achievements without being obnoxious?"), but a little bit of "internal marketing" can't harm, especially if your Dean and VC are also following you ☺.

## Blogs: staying up to date with the academic world

Finally, blogs can be a really good way to stay up to date with what is happening in the academic world. I find following blogs such as LSE's Impact of Social Sciences Blog (see screenshot below), Wonkhe, and the Scholarly Kitchen very useful. They are generally written "by academics for academics" and provide reliable information about many aspects of academic life.

### The Accelerated Academy Series

Now a symptom of that which it sought to critique? A critical reflection on the Accelerated Academy project

Despite becoming increasingly institutionalised, there remains a lack of discourse about research metrics among much of academia

How are academic lives sustained? Gender and the ethics of care in the neoliberal accelerated academy

You might also want to follow some blogs by your main professional associations. The *Academy of Management* for instance has an Ethics blog where academics can "discuss ethical issues that affect their research, teaching and professional lives". The *Academy of International Business* also has an Ethics blog. I even wrote a guest post for it on how to keep your Google Scholar Profile clean (see below). Ask your colleagues for tips about useful blogs to follow.

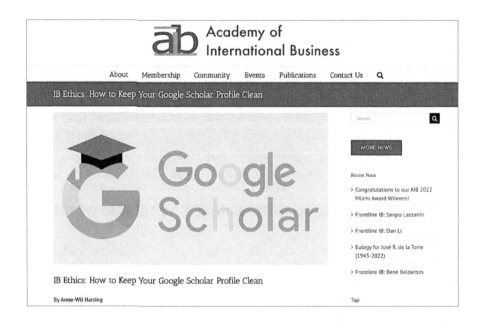

IB Ethics: How to Keep Your Google Scholar Profile Clean

By Anne-Wil Harzing                                      Tags

I would love it if more academics blogged about their own research, especially if they have published a significant body of work on a topic. Academics are increasingly time-poor, so blogposts provide a great introduction to someone's research.

For instance, rather than read half a dozen of my articles about each of these topics: language barriers in multinationals, country-of-origin effects in multinationals, and diversity in editorial boards, you could just read my integrative blogposts summarising these research streams. They could help you decide whether you wanted to dig deeper and read the actual papers.

## Sharing (news about) your research

As I have discussed in previous chapters, several of the social media platforms (LinkedIn, Twitter, and Blogging) are very well suited to share news about your research. ResearchGate can also be used for this purpose if you use their "project" feature. Moreover, it is ideally suited to host full-text versions of your papers to easily disseminate your work.

The video featured below provides a detailed overview of the seven steps to follow to improve the chances that your latest paper reaches its desired audience. This doesn't have to take up a huge amount of your time, it takes me 6-16 hours per paper. Does that sound like a lot to you? Maybe... But given how much work you have put into doing the research and writing the paper, why wouldn't you devote 1-2 more days ensuring it gets the audience it deserves?

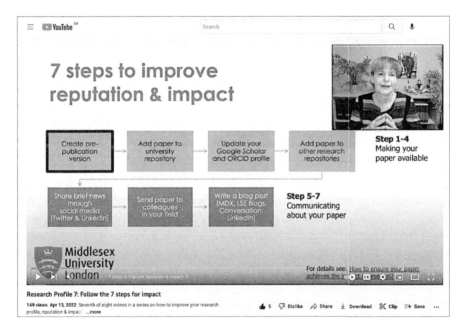

## Write once, share many times

One way to ensure you make the most of your efforts, is to use social media platforms in a complementary fashion so they reinforce each other. If you have invested a lot of time writing something up nicely, or have written something that is core to your current job or research interests, make sure you share it through different channels.

A few years ago, I wrote up a blogpost about my role in creating an inclusive research culture at Middlesex University Business School. This blogpost was re-posted on Middlesex Minds; I also shared it as an article on LinkedIn. Subsequently, I tweeted about it and pinned this tweet to my Twitter account for a while (see below).

Once you have a store of blogposts that are time-less (which most of my own blogposts are) you can periodically re-share them on Twitter and LinkedIn. As views and engagements on both platforms depend heavily on whether your followers are looking at their timelines at that point in time, sharing a carefully crafted post just once is a waste of your precious time.

I wouldn't recommend sharing the same post several times a day – although some people do – or even several times a week, but sharing useful posts half a dozen times a year is certainly not overkill. And you can always include your favourite posts or shares in your email signature. Here is one of mine where I did this.

**Prof. Anne-Wil Harzing**
Professor of International Management
Middlesex University London, Business School
Fellow of the Academy of International Business

**Web:** Harzing.com - **Twitter:** @awharzing - **Google Scholar:** Citation Profile
Celebrating CYGNA: Supporting women in academia
Creating a supportive & collaborative research culture at Middlesex University Business School

*Please note that due to my working pattern you may sometimes get emails from me outside of normal working hours. Please do NOT feel obliged to respond outside of your own usual working hours.*

More generally, you can improve your effectiveness in academia by applying the "write once, refine through repetition, then use many times" principle more widely. This book is an updated and extended version of an 8-part blogpost series on academic social media use. In turn these blogposts derived from presentations given at Middlesex and other universities on the "how and why" of using social media in academia, as well as several hands-on "social media clinics". So, rather than limiting the reach of this carefully crafted material only to the people who attended the seminars and clinics, it made sense to spend a bit more time to convert it into something I could share with everyone.

## In sum

This final chapter recapped the strengths and use cases for the five social platforms we discussed in detail in Chapters 2-7. I hope this book has given you a taste of how social media can be useful in supporting your academic career.

# Conclusion

In this book I first provided a primer on social media in academia (Chapter 1), compared key options (Chapter 2), and provided tips for five key social media platforms: Google Scholar Profiles (Chapter 3), LinkedIn (Chapter 4), ResearchGate (Chapter 5), Twitter (Chapter 6), and Blogging (Chapter 7). Chapter 8 recapped the strengths of the five different platforms by considering two key use areas: the use of social media as a source of professional/academic information and the use of social media to share (news about) your research.

I hope this guide has helped to demystify the topic of social media in academia and provided you with the tools to be successful in your social media efforts. I would love to hear from you if you feel it has helped you; feel free to get in touch with me at anne@harzing.com.

Remember though that none of what we have discussed in this book is a "once and for ever" choice. You can always change or finetune your social media presence. Moreover, do take a break from social media for a few weeks or a few months if your work is busy or you just want to hide in your own little world for a while. We all have periods like that. Nothing is compulsory.

Your social media engagement should be meaningful to *you*, don't engage in mindless scrolling or frantic exchanges as it won't do your mental health any good. Even more so than when using social media privately, when using it professionally it should really be purposeful. Make it work for *you*, don't let yourself be driven by the platforms.

# Further reading

My blog contains many more posts related to social media, as well as academic careers more generally. Below I have reproduced a partial list, structured by topic. Just Google the title and you will find them easily.

## Social media

**Social Media in Academia (1): Introduction**
16 Jan 2020 – Anne-Wil Harzing
An introduction into my 8-part blogpost series on social media

**Social Media in Academia (2): Comparing the options**
28 Jan 2020 – Anne-Wil Harzing
General recommendations on how to use social media professionally

**Social Media in Academia (3): Google Scholar Profiles**
10 Feb 2020 – Anne-Wil Harzing
Provides recommendations on how to get the best out of Google Scholar Profiles

**Social Media in Academia (4): LinkedIn**
27 Feb 2020 – Anne-Wil Harzing
Provides recommendations on how to get the best out of LinkedIn

**Social media in Academia (5): ResearchGate**
09 Mar 2020 – Anne-Wil Harzing
Provides recommendations on how to get the most out of ResearchGate

**Social Media in Academia (6): Twitter**
27 Mar 2020 – Anne-Wil Harzing
Provides recommendations on how to get the best out of Twitter

### Social media in Academia (7): Blogging
13 Apr 2020 – Anne-Wil Harzing
Provides recommendations on how to start with blogging

### Social Media in Academia (8): Putting it all together
27 Apr 2020 – Anne-Wil Harzing
Final posting in the social media series explains how different social media can reinforce each other

### Social Media in Academia: Using LinkedIn to promote your research
08 Apr 2021 – Christa Sathish
Tips and tricks for using LinkedIn to promote your research

### How to digitally market yourself: a beginner's guide for students and academics
06 Nov 2021 – Christa Sathish
Handy tips and tricks to start building a digital presence

---

# Publishing

### The four P's of getting published
08 Dec 2016 – Anne-Wil Harzing
Short summary of my white paper explaining how performance, practice, participation, and persistence are needed in publishing academic papers

### The four ailments of academic writing and how to cure them
20 Apr 2020 – Nico Pizzolato
Some golden tips on how to improve your academic writing

### How to keep up-to-date with the literature, but avoid information overload?
14 May 2018 – Anne-Wil Harzing
Provides tips on how to keep up-to-date without getting lost

## How many references is enough?
30 May 2020 – Anne-Wil Harzing
Some reflections on why more references isn't always better, but how strategic referencing might help

## CYGNA: Writing a literature review paper: whether, what, and when?
19 Sep 2021 – Anne-Wil Harzing
Reports on our 41st CYGNA meeting on the challenge of publishing literature review papers

## Want to publish a literature review? Think of it as an empirical paper
23 Apr 2021 – Tatiana Andreeva
What to consider if you want to publish a literature review paper

## How to avoid a desk-reject in seven steps [1/8]
10 May 2020 – Anne-Wil Harzing
Introduces a 7-step process to increase your chances of getting your paper into the review process

## Who do you want to talk to? Targeting journals [2/8]
24 May 2020 – Anne-Wil Harzing
Explains why choosing your target journal is the most important step in the publication process

## Your title: the public face of your paper [3/8]
14 Jun 2020 – Anne-Wil Harzing
Illustrates how to create a good title through an iterative process

## Writing your abstract: not a last-minute activity [4/8]
28 Jun 2020 – Anne-Wil Harzing
Explains what needs to be included in an effective abstract

## Your introduction: first impressions count! [5/8]
11 Sep 2020 – Anne-Wil Harzing
What are the elements of an effective introduction: context, importance, and interest

**Conclusions: last impressions count too! [6/8]**
18 Sep 2020 – Anne-Wil Harzing
Why conclusions are a crucial part of your paper's key message

**What do you cite? Using references strategically [7/8]**
03 Oct 2020 – Anne-Wil Harzing
Shows you how references can save you hundreds of words and position your paper

**Why do I need to write a letter to the editor? [8/8]**
16 Oct 2020 – Anne-Wil Harzing
The last step in the submission process is an important means to "sell" your paper to the journal

**From little seed to fully-grown tree: a paper development journey**
09 May 2022 – Heejin Kim
A novice publisher providing a "behind the scenes" look at co-authoring for top journals

**CYGNA: The wonderful world of book publishing**
12 Dec 2020 – Anne-Wil Harzing
Reports on our 35th CYGNA meeting with three publishers discussing textbooks, research books and practice books

**Own your place in the world by writing a book**
11 Dec 2018 – Nico Pizzolato
A passionate plea to consider publishing a book at least once in your academic career

**IB Frontline interview: mentoring section**
03 Jan 2022 – Anne-Wil Harzing
Introduces the third section of my IB Frontline interview talking about my role as a mentor and my top tips for early career researchers

# Career progression

**CYGNA: Internal versus External promotion**
11 Oct 2018 – Anne-Wil Harzing
Reports on our 22nd CYGNA meeting with a presentation giving tips for internal and external promotion applications

**CYGNA: climbing up the academic career ladder**
03 May 2021 – Anne-Wil Harzing
Reports on our 39th CYGNA meeting with a focus on career progression

**CYGNA: How do I keep my job (in academia) in uncertain times?**
13 Nov 2020 – Anne-Wil Harzing
Reports on our 34th CYGNA meeting discussing jobs losses in higher education in COVID-19 times

**CYGNA: One size doesn't fit all – Diversity of academic career paths**
28 Feb 2022 – Anne-Wil Harzing
Reports on our 45th CYGNA meeting in which we discussed four alternative career paths in academia

**Open Syllabus Explorer: evidencing research-based teaching?**
15 Nov 2019 – Anne-Wil Harzing
Reviews how the Open Syllabus Project can help academics to understand their impact on teaching and find the best textbook for their course

**Presenting your case for tenure or promotion?**
23 Nov 2016 – Anne-Wil Harzing
Shows how to make your case for tenure or promotion by comparing your record to a relevant peer group

**How to create a sustainable academic career**
21 Nov 2020 – Anne-Wil Harzing
Reports on Martyna Sliwa's presentation on career progression in the UK higher education environment

## How to create a successful academic career: AIB – Ask, Invest & Believe
22 Jun 2019 – Anne-Wil Harzing
Write-up of my contribution to a conference panel on career strategies at the 2017 AIB-UKI meeting in Birmingham

## CV of failures
15 Jun 2019 – Anne-Wil Harzing
Explains why rejection and failure are a normal part of an academic career and not something to hide or be embarrassed about

## Publish or Perish increases transparency in academic appointments
14 Oct 2016 – Anne-Wil Harzing
Illustrates how PoP has been used to expose nepotism and incompetence

## CYGNA: Careers, mobility and belonging: foreign women academics in the UK
02 Jun 2018 – Anne-Wil Harzing
Reports on our 15th CYGNA meeting with a special emphasis on the challenges for female foreign academics in the UK

## Why are there so few female Economics professors?
11 Nov 2018 – Anne-Wil Harzing
Short summary of my article in Economisch Statistische Berichten on gender bias and meritocracy in academia

## We need a different kind of superhero: improving gender diversity in academia
12 Jan 2021 – Jill A. Gould
Collects the resources developed for the 2020 AoM symposium on creating gender inclusive academic environments

## WAIB Panel: Academic career strategies for women in the UK
01 May 2018 – Anne-Wil Harzing
Reports on a WAIB Panel at the AIB-UKI meeting in Birmingham April 2018

# Research impact and funding

**The four C's of getting cited**
18 Sep 2017 – Anne-Wil Harzing
Short summary of white paper explaining why competence, collaboration, care, and communication help to realise the citation impact of your work

**Everything you always wanted to know about impact...**
02 Jun 2019 – Anne-Wil Harzing
Book chapter providing a quick overview of the what, why, how and where of research impact

**How to ensure your paper achieves the impact it deserves?**
15 Jan 2018 – Anne-Wil Harzing
Discusses the workflow I use to communicate about a new paper

**Impact is impact is impact? Well, no...**
20 Jun 2022 – Anne-Wil Harzing
Reprint of an invited blogpost on the SAGE Social Science Space on disambiguating the concept of impact

**Research Academics as Change Makers – Opportunities and Barriers**
13 Nov 2021 – Andrea Werner
Reports on a Middlesex University panel discussion on creating external research impact

**How to make your case for impact?**
13 Jul 2016 – Anne-Wil Harzing
Shows you how to make your case for impact by comparing your papers to the journal average

**Making your case for impact if you have few citations**
27 Nov 2017 – Anne-Wil Harzing
Provides advice on strategies to demonstrate impact with a very low citation level

### How to find your next research project?
16 Jun 2016 – Anne-Wil Harzing
Provides suggestions on how to find new and interesting research projects

### CYGNA: Working in a Horizon-2020 project
19 Feb 2021 – Anne-Wil Harzing
Reports on our 37th CYGNA meeting dealing with research funding and working in large, funded projects

### How to write successful funding applications?
02 Nov 2016 – Anne-Wil Harzing
Provides ten tips for successful funding applications

### Finding a Unicorn? Research funding in Business & Management research
05 May 2019 – Anne-Wil Harzing
Explains why university administrators need to be realistic in the amount of research funding they can expect Business School academics to generate

### CYGNA: Positionality, team roles, and academic activism
27 Jun 2022 – Anne-Wil Harzing
Reports on our 47th CYGNA meeting, celebrating our 8-year anniversary with our first face-to-face meeting in 2.5 years

## Other academic skills

### Be proactive, resilient & realistic!
07 Jan 2020 – Anne-Wil Harzing
Argues that as an academic you are an independent professional shaping your own career

### How to prevent burn-out? About staying sane in academia
12 May 2016 – Anne-Wil Harzing
Provides twelve suggestions on how to prevent burn-out and keep your sanity

**CYGNA: Work intensification, well-being and career advancement**
08 Dec 2019 – Anne-Wil Harzing
Reports on our 29th CYGNA meeting dealing with workloads and work intensification

**On academic life: collaborations and active engagement**
19 Jun 2018 – Anne-Wil Harzing
Discusses Martyna Sliwa's articles on the different rationalities underlying research collaborations and the need to get involved in managing and shaping the university organisations we work for

**Want to impress at an academic job interview?**
24 Jan 2017 – Anne-Wil Harzing
Shows you how to use PoP do some intelligence gathering to make a good impression at a job interview

**CYGNA: Working effectively with support staff in academia**
06 Mar 2018 – Anne-Wil Harzing
Reports on our 18th CYGNA meeting with a presentation on working with support staff and a discussion of boundaryless careers

**CYGNA: Life-long learning in academia**
03 Apr 2019 – Anne-Wil Harzing
Reports on our 25th CYGNA meeting with presentations on an Erasmus visit and participation in the Aurora program

**How to hold on to your sanity in academia**
11 Apr 2019 – Steffi Siegert
Steffi Siegert's powerful contribution that sums up everything that women can be facing in academia

**CYGNA: Negotiation workshop**
15 Feb 2020 – Anne-Wil Harzing
Reports on our 30th CYGNA meeting dealing with negotiation styles

**How to promote your research achievements without being obnoxious?**
01 Dec 2018 – Anne-Wil Harzing
Provides some quick and easy to implement tips on how to promote your academic work

**CYGNA: Resistance to gender equality in academia**
15 Mar 2021 – Anne-Wil Harzing
Reports on our 38th CYGNA meeting dealing with one of the ultimate gender topics

**What is that conference networking thing all about?**
01 Nov 2017 – Anne-Wil Harzing
Reflections on the importance of networking in academia and tips on how to do it

**CYGNA: Supervising and being supervised**
02 May 2022 – Anne-Wil Harzing
Reports on our 46th CYGNA meeting where we discussed our experiences of PhD supervision, both from a student and from a supervisor perspective

**Meeting an official guest or your academic hero?**
15 Sep 2016 – Anne-Wil Harzing
Shows you how to prepare for any academic meeting in 5-10 minutes